Playing to
WIN
or Afraid to
LOSE

Playing to
WIN
or Afraid to
LOSE

*Stepping Up and
Stepping Into Sales*

CHARLES BARRETT

ARCHWAY
PUBLISHING

Archway Publishing books may be ordered through booksellers or by contacting:

Archway Publishing
1663 Liberty Drive
Bloomington, IN 47403
www.archwaypublishing.com
1 (888) 242-5904

ISBN: 978-1-4808-8238-6 (sc)
ISBN: 978-1-4808-8237-9 (hc)
ISBN: 978-1-4808-8239-3 (e)

Library of Congress Control Number: 2019915232

Print information available on the last page.

Archway Publishing rev. date: 10/16/2019

Acknowledgments

I have to thank Tom Brennan for doing yeoman's work in taking all my handwritten notes/copy and putting together the first full draft of this book. Tom should be applauded for deciphering my handwriting alone. Tom was so enthusiastic about this project from beginning to end.

A huge thank you to Sue Warner (professional editor) who crafted the initial draft into a working book. She added all those professional touches that only an expert can. Thank you as well goes to Sue for her patience, guidance and understanding dealing with a person like me who has never written a book before.

Many thanks go to Joe Cozza with whom, over the years, I have discussed many of the sales concepts outlined in this book, as well as the critical importance of customer relationships and that all-important concept of "Trust" these relationships require.

Thank you, as well, to my lovely wife Joy and our daughter Sandra who both constantly encouraged me throughout the entire (lengthy) process. I admit there were times I just didn't think we would get there. On the technological side of things, my sons CJ and Tim always stepped in and lent assistance to me – the technologically challenged – when asked .And a very special thanks to Luke Liao who (not once but twice and only on one hour notice) drove over to my house to extricate me from self-inflicted technological problems I was having at very critical times in the completion of this project.

A special thanks to my son, Christopher, who took after Dad and got into the food and beverage industry. Chris has provided me with both inspiration and support from the beginning to the end of this entire endeavor. What's even nicer about that is I don't think he even realized it.

Last, but certainly not least—a big thank you to Nick Katsoris. Nick is a highly successful lawyer and an equally successful author in his own right and was so enthusiastic and encouraging to me when I first approached him with my idea about writing this book.

Contents

Introduction

This is not a typical book; it is more a reference manual or resource guide. By definition, a resource guide is something you would come back to often to reference specific topics. The idea is to initially take a few concepts and implement them now; a kind of "Take what you want and leave the rest for another day" approach.

My aim is to provide both the novice and the seasoned sales professional with a written step-by-step guideline that covers the entire sales process in detail and in chronological order (as much as possible) and to articulate with real-life examples the key fundamentals of selling. There are mental, emotional and physical requirements if you want to have a highly successful career in sales. We will go into a very thorough explanation and analysis of those requirements.

Although the material presented is applicable to many other fields – e.g., real estate, consumer products, finance, insurance – its specific focus is catering and event sales. This book provides the reader with a very logical and easy to follow approach to what you need to know, what you need to think, and what you need to do every day to develop the most highly effective, most proactive selling skills possible.

This manual is not written from the vantage point of someone in a corporate office (or to use a bit of corporate jargon— "from 30,000 feet up"). No, it is written totally from the perspective of someone on the ground – someone who has worked extensively in the field. It is written from my vantage point as a highly experienced salesperson who spent his entire career prospecting/soliciting new business, as well as developing /growing existing accounts and competing for catering and events business in by far the most competitive and largest revenue grossing catering market in the country – New York City.

I can almost hear a naysayer or two right now saying, "Oh, this is just one of those motivational books." Not quite. It is predominantly an instructional guide. I will share my own personal experiences (from working in five different venues) as well as others' learnings and experiences that have been shared with me to highlight major themes throughout. To the point of being a motivational resource, I will point you towards a very famous salesperson – Mr. Zig Ziglar – who said, "People often say motivation doesn't last. Well, neither does bathing; that's why we recommend it daily."[1] There's a lot of "daily" in sales as you will see shortly.

This manual covers over 90% of what you will encounter in selling. Why not 100%? The only reason I say that is I don't think any book can ever cover it all. Several of the examples I use reflect mistakes I personally have made. I can point to other examples and say I have made similar errors in judgment. You don't learn if you don't try. Thankfully, I have learned, changed and grown throughout my career. So, you, the reader, can look at this book knowing I have saved you a huge amount of time, frustration and disappointment. I have already made most of the mistakes for you.

Selling, for some odd reason, has always been one of those professions about which everybody (who does not work directly in sales) seems to have an opinion. Of course, they are not the ones doing the selling. If you have been in the selling profession for even a brief period of time you probably already know much of what others tell you usually does not play out that way at all.

So, we are going to be talking about the truth of selling – straight talk – to counter so many of those hackneyed myths about selling and salespeople. You will have the benefit of a very well researched analysis and guided approach to making sales. And along the way, you will be challenged to honestly analyze your own sales skills, practices and assumptions.

To be candid, many novice salespeople (and, unfortunately, some with years of experience) just don't know how to professionally and

---

[1] Brainyquote.com

skillfully approach a potential customer – much less an existing customer – with any sense of confidence. Yes, they have all taken a few sales training courses. However, I think we have to own up to the fact that sometimes the material and the examples offered in those courses are just not germane to our everyday sales world. Adding to this disconnect, some of the sales trainers themselves come from a mostly reactive sales background. How do you train someone to be proactive if you have not had the experience (or enough of an experience) in the field yourself? How do you train someone to enter very competitive markets when your own experience is in fairly stable, reactive ones?

Another aspect of sales this manual will address is salespeople who constantly tell you their type of selling is somehow completely different, special and unique from the rest of the industry, and even different from similar venues in their city. This kind of thinking, of course, short circuits the need to do any analysis of one's own sales skills. It conveniently allows for the salesperson to live within what I call the self-inflicted "Illusion of Selling." It is their "go to" excuse to rationalize their own lack of thought and commitment to their profession.

So often I've heard: "Our business is different; it's all reactive," or, "It all comes in over the phone," or "All we get are RFPs. People do not have time to talk, they want everything by email." I have several thoughts on how to navigate through this quagmire, which I will get into in the following pages. However, first I would ask you to challenge yourself: Where do you expect to be in your career in two years or three years? Where will you be in five or six years? Presumably, you will be moving into positions/venues that are more varied and will require more of you, in terms of communication, presentation skills and sales sophistication. Your daily interactions, therefore, will evolve from being more hands-on/reactive to being much more long range and strategically driven.

In other words, your career should move along on a continuum from being 100% totally reactive to being almost 70% proactive selling. This is a continuum, along which, your customers, their needs and their events will become increasingly more intricate, more nuanced. Your level of professional interaction with these customers and their expectations of you will similarly need to evolve to a much higher and more mature standard. We will look at all of this and provide you with some constructive answers and techniques to get you in the game.

My approach to selling catering and events is not theoretical in the least. It is a proven winning formula, based on extensive experience and daily application of the principles and habits you will encounter in reading this book. My attitude is premised on several constructs and disciplines which – if consistently practiced and incorporated into your daily routine – will ensure you much more consistent success and a decidedly more lucrative catering and event sales experience.

The Commodity Myth

Many customers think of catering as basically a commodity. To them, competing products and venues are pretty much indistinguishable from each other. As a result, these buyers often choose on the basis of almost exclusively price alone – *the lowest price*. They have relatively low expectations, are generally skeptical in their approach and are much less sensitive to and cognizant of differences in competing venues. Their main concern is for quick, easy, one-dimensional transactions. In other words, they are not engaged. Inexperienced and ineffective salespeople assume the same thing, and thereby reinforce this commodity mindset by their knee-jerk reaction: constantly cutting price. Advances in technology not only support but further exacerbates this commodity mindset. This one-dimensional type of behavior undermines both the salesperson's and the product's credibility and brand. When you reduce yourself to competing on price, you define yourself as a commodity.

Great catering salespeople know better. They see the customer relationship as a multi-dimensional, ever-moving and evolving experience; in other words, a true relationship. And this approach reaps them big rewards, both in the short and long term. Look at Starbucks. They created an experience – a value proposition – that transcended price. They set a price point that reflected this value proposition and they interacted with/ educated their consumers to rethink the importance of a daily coffee break. We will talk a lot more about how the same applies in catering.

One of the most important takeaways for the reader of this book will be: How you can challenge the commodity mindset and avoid commodity status. How do you sidestep being engulfed in this vicious cycle to begin with? How do you find a way to engage or re-engage a buyer who is locked into this kind of tunnel vision? And, in some cases, do you even bother?

RISK TAKERS

Entrepreneurs, small business owners and many immigrants are the true risk takers in our country.[2] They see possibilities and opportunities and are not afraid to proactively jump into a business and give it their all. They become adept at picking up cues that signal misunderstanding or mistrust. They become very good at reading people and noticing the relationships between people. If they fail. they fail quickly, so they can move on to success. This is a vital mindset. By contrast, those in more established companies can be lulled into seeing the business landscape as almost static, instead of filled with unlimited potential. Entrepreneurs focus on strategies to win over customers. Conversely, in more established companies the temptation for many is to hide behind processes to deal with customers while calling these "strategies" to win customers. The risk-averse say things like, "What if" or "I don't think we can do ...." True risk-takers say, "So what?" and "I'm going for it." You will learn more about how to approach your catering sales career with the same hungry small business owner/entrepreneur mindset.

Some salespeople are so risk averse that they create an illusion they are "selling" when, in fact, they are doing nothing of the kind. All their selling is founded on the law of averages – kind of like selling based on the lowest common denominator. This attitude is a sales non-starter.

---

[2] The Kaufman Foundation's annual index of Startup Activity shows that immigrants to the United States were almost twice as likely as native-born Americans to start a new business in the United States in 2016. Almost 30% of all new entrepreneurs are immigrants. A total of 40.2% of Fortune 500 companies have at least one founder who either immigrated to the United States or whose parents were immigrants. Fortune 500 companies started by immigrants employ over 13.6 million people.

To be a successful salesperson you have to get out of your comfort zone and confront the issues. In sales, you always have to be comfortable with being slightly uncomfortable. I will reference and develop this theme often as we move through this book.

SALES IS A SPORT

Classic sales books and training classes support this premise, but mostly as a metaphor. I am talking about selling though as literally a "contact sport." You've got to be an active participant – a player, not an observer. Sales has physical, mental and emotional components, and just like any other athlete, you've got to make the commitment to train, to practice. I will go into greater detail about this and how you can train yourself into strong sales habits.

Case in point: Your average amateur tennis player does not move his feet enough nor quickly enough. He tends to be late seeing where the ball is going and, as a result, tends to go for low percentage shots to counter his missteps.[3] There is an underlying tenseness and lack of focus in his game. We will see how all this plays into and applies to selling and what you can do to counter it.

I play tennis and golf, both of which offer apt analogies, as do football, basketball – really any contact sport. We "weekend warriors" connect on a very personal level to imperatives, such as "take the ball early," "go for it," "commit to the shot," don't think, play" and "finish the point decisively." If you already play a sport and, better yet, compete (or even if you regularly challenge yourself while exercising in a gym or health club), you will automatically relate to these analogies. And by the way, there is much more going on out there on a tennis court than just two people hitting a ball back and forth over a net.

Kobe Bryant once said (and I am paraphrasing), most of the other players out there are playing checkers.... I'm playing chess. This is right in line with what this manual is all about: Taking your game up several

---

[3] Throughout this book, I will use the pronoun "his" or "he" when referring to a customer or salesperson, to avoid the awkward "he or she," "him or her" phrasing.

notches to "that" level. It's about having a much broader vision – a stronger sense of where you want to be 10 or 12 steps later in the sales process. This is where you want to play the game – at that level and with the kind of confidence and intensity Kobe Bryant is depicting. I will show you examples to bring that point home.

Whereas Kobe Bryant alluded to a key intangible sales skill, pro golfer Lee Trevino spoke directly to it. He said it is an absolute necessity if you are going to be an indispensable performer, "There is no such thing as natural touch. Touch is something you create by hitting millions of golf balls."[4] You rarely, if ever, read anything about this in a sales book, and yet in the field of sports you will hear constant references to "a good sense of touch." This is one of the great intangible skills of selling – trusting your gut instincts. Although this phrase almost implies this is something you are either born with or not, that's not really true. You can learn it. Practice, Practice, Practice! This is one of the main mantras of this manual. If you do, you will develop a very good feel for this game we call sales.

Both entrepreneurs and those who play sports know that when you have a good feel for the game, you can move about the court with ease, even when you have only about 50 to 70% of the information. Even without complete information, you can still sense when to step into action and when not to. It is a letting go and sensing where the game is moving. I have always referred to it as being comfortable "living in the gray." Many aren't, and these folks do not belong in sales. Those who are comfortable with "the gray" usually excel.

Any good salesperson is a performer. The great ones know it and thrive on it. For them it is like performing on a high wire without a net. In golf, the caddy might help with club selection and advice on how to play a particular shot, but in the end, it is the player who has to make the shot, the one who has to make it happen. To succeed in sports, you have to be relaxed, believe in yourself, trust yourself and be focused only on that ball. In this manual you will learn how to adapt and apply these concepts, how to work your plan, how to author your shots and how you can dictate play and win.

---

[4] brainyquotes.com

Stretching the truth or outright lying can come easy in sales – too easy for some. What do you personally do every day to stay honest with yourself? Are you deceiving yourself by buying into corporate speak or are you talking with your customers and prospective customers as real human beings? It all starts with the latter.

Athletes are very candid about their performance—they openly acknowledge mistakes made and opportunities not seized upon. In sales, though, there is a tendency for some to default to what I call the all motion is progress game. It fits right in with the illusion of selling dynamic I just referenced. These salespeople immerse themselves in "doing things" (anything) with little thought as to if their actions have any true bearing on realistically driving sales. The focus is all on a frenetic amount of activity …….not on results. And, being very honest, it is based in fear not confidence. The antidote to this will always be getting honest with yourself.

In this book, I employ the term "absolute honesty." The reality of sales is right in line with the well-worn (for good reason) "80/20 Rule": 80% of an outcome is due to 20% of the action. Applied to sales, you can say that about 80% of your total sales are produced by the top 20% of your salesforce. Even fewer salespeople (5%) are indispensable performers. I will show you how candor – getting honest with yourself and others and being committed to the principle of absolute honesty – is one of the main ingredients to becoming an indispensable catering sales performer.

WINNING

Do Novak Djokovic or Serena Williams aspire to be the President of the World Team Tennis Association? Does Dustin Johnson want to be the President of the Professional Golfers Association? Does the principal star in any Broadway show aspire to be the Director of Administration of the theater? The answer in all cases is: highly unlikely. He or she wants to be spoken and written about as the #1 performer/player in his or her profession. Wanting to be #1, wanting to be the indispensable and outstanding performer on your team – that is the overwhelming subject and message of this book.

Roger Federer said it best: "As much as I am content and happy to be playing, you need the fire, you need to want to achieve things. As much as I love everything around me, at the end of the day I'm here to win." [5] Winners agree with and don't shy away from Roger's statement, but not average sales performers. Why? Because they are busy thinking: "What if I *don't* win?"

Today, in everyday life, we tend to hear all too often, "Everyone is Great!" "Everyone is a Winner!" "Everybody gets a chance!" These statements have replaced, "The best rise to the top!" So often, it can seem like people are being rewarded for just fitting in versus really standing out. The reality, as coach Bobby Knight said, is:

> *"If everybody is a winner, then no one is a winner.*
> *There is a word for that – we call it a tie."* [6]

Knight went on to say:

> *"Good is the enemy of great, because if we are*
> *too easily satisfied, we lose our edge."* [7]

And William Gilbert put it perfectly over 120 years ago:

> *"When everyone is somebody then no one's anybody."* [8]

Throughout your reading you will encounter examples of order takers and untrained salespeople, as well as those wonderful peak performers. I will talk about what the differences are between them. I will also address how you get there and what separates the winners from

---

[5] New York Times Magazine –Michael Steinberger—August 23, 2013

[6] New York Post –Michael Kane – March 3, 2013

[7] New York Post—Michael Kane—March 3, 2013

[8] "The Gondoliers," W. S. Gilbert libretto, 1889

the "losers" and "also-rans." I have found many salespeople are uncomfortable hearing those and similar terms. They shy away from making such bold statements. Being honest though – and this is what sales is all about – is crucial. Robert Kiyosaki summed it up very aptly...and I am only partially quoting him on this –"Winners are not afraid of losing; but losers are."

I have given extensive coverage and focus to the first two chapters of this resource guide. These chapters outline what I call the essential core of selling. The core comprises the Four Pillars (the framework) and the Six Habits (the six critical "must haves") that form the very foundation and launching pad for whatever success you will have in the field. They are:

THE 4 PILLARS	THE 6 HABITS
Needs...Wants	The Knowledge Habit
Listen...then Question	The Connecting Habit
Like vs. Trust	The (Probing) Questioning Habit
Fear... to Belief... to Winning	The Managing Time Habit
	The Doing the Little Things Habit
	The Regenerating Habit

The requirements, as I have said, are at once mental, physical and emotional; the mental game being the most important. All the chapters that follow – from prospecting/ solicitation/ networking through meeting with a potential customer, submitting a proposal and negotiating and closing the business, align with these critically important Pillars and Habits. Throughout, I provide real-life (not generic) examples from the field to highlight key points – another benefit to the reader, since all examples are relevant and applicable to anyone working in the field.

The best salespeople absolutely love what they do – they fully embrace their profession, they make things happen, they keep it simple, and they make sure they never conduct themselves in the all-too-typical "just another salesperson" mode. As Mary Kay Ash so eloquently summed it up:

> *"Life is a Banquet and most poor sons-of-bitches are starving to death."*[9]

THE STORY OF THE SHOTGUN SALESPERSON

The short story I am about to outline is what I would call (very broadly speaking) a statement of what currently transpires for many salespeople when a prospective customer arrives at their door. It sets the stage for all that is to follow. The challenge for you is to honestly refer back to this story (as you go through this manual) and candidly acknowledge where you have done similar things. Is this story repeated in full by all salespeople every day? No. However, this story does occur more often than you would think, and for some more often than for others. We will address how you can change your behavior to avoid such outcomes. So, as you review this story, put aside that all-too-natural defensiveness we all seem to have and remain open and willing to listen to some important alternatives.

So, as a prelude to the first chapter of this book, I am going to outline a sales scenario, which I think we can all relate to: The Shotgun Sales Approach. The predominate characteristic of this style is "scattered" – slightly scattered to very scattered to essentially winging it – versus a more targeted, more precise approach. All of us have "shot gunned it" on occasion. Why? Because many times, it works...for reactive sales. For instance, when you already know and have a past history with the organization or corporation that calls in and wants to book a program with you, odds are they will book with you if, for no other reason, they have used your facility several times before. You did not actively pursue their business. Or, their company has an established relationship with your company on a national basis and, per their senior leadership team,

---

[9] From "Auntie Mame" stage play (1956), based on the novel by Patrick Dennis.

are instructed to use your venue as much as possible. So, if you are a little bit or even very scattered, it doesn't have that much of a negative impact. You are probably going to get the business in spite of your less-than-stellar sales skills.

The shotgun approach works just often enough that you can convince yourself it will work most, if not all, of the time. The thing is, it doesn't work all the time or, should I say, it doesn't work on the really big important sales, those that give you the biggest thrill and sense of accomplishment, that ultimate sense of winning we all want to feel. The shotgun sales approach doesn't work with the more proactive kinds of sales where a corporation or an organization is visiting three or four different facilities, securing and evaluating proposals from each, and then coming to a decision for their event after a very careful and critical analysis of the pros and cons of each facility.

Falling back on the shotgun approach in these more critical situations usually isn't intentional. Most of us want to do a good job. We have good intentions. What happens though is we get caught-up in all those little interruptions that occur every day. We get caught up in those minor "emergencies" – the ones that are always disguised as real emergencies. As a result, we don't properly plan and prepare; we don't get ahead of the situation; we don't set ourselves up to win. Just like in tennis or any other competitive sport, if you have not done the proper stretching warmup prior to the game and/or if your physical set up is incorrect, no matter how hard you try, the end result will be the same: Failure. You'll hit the ball wide, long or into the net.

So, what happens? Let's take a look at Bob. Bob has an appointment scheduled for 10 a.m. He decides to get into work a little early that morning to prepare himself. But then he gets a call from his operational staff telling him there is a little problem with a large group of his taking place right now. So, he rushes out to see what he can do. After talking with his customer and operational staff, Bob resolves the problem and heads back to his office to prepare for his appointment. But just then, his boss strolls in and says, "Hey do you have a minute?" A minute turns into 25 minutes while Bob's boss "thinks out loud" with him regarding some pressing corporate challenge that just can't seem to wait.

I think you get the picture. Suddenly the receptionist calls; Bob's appointment is here. So, what does he do? He quickly grabs a few brochures, floor plans and a menu kit and goes to reception to greet his prospect. Although he has a forced smile on his face, if you really look closely (and most customers are looking closely), Bob's face betrays an underlying sense of strain and fear. He knows he is not prepared, and it shows. Oh, he knows a few basic facts and information about the event, but deep down, he realizes he isn't fully prepared. But, hey, he's not going to let that get in the way. Bob launches into a very perfunctory, shaking of hands, and a breathy, quick hello to everyone. He sounds like he's out of breath, as though he'd been running. His body language and voice are sending several messages: He's a little bit nervous, anxious, jumpy. Translation: Bob's unsure of himself, and it's likely that these non-verbal messages are being conveyed before he's even said a word.

Bob's next big mistake: He doesn't bother to suggest sitting down in the conference room to review a few details before taking a tour or, at best, he sits down for a very cursory, superficial discussion. Plowing ahead, he then looks at everybody and says, "Well, shall we take a look?" Fatal mistake.

Off he goes with essentially no idea what he is doing or why. So, instead of Bob being in control of the sales process, the prospect is in control – pulling Bob in all sorts of directions and shooting a variety of questions at him from all corners and in random order. He is being led instead of leading. He is following along, not presenting. When challenged, such a salesperson will invariably say that the customer did not have time for a lengthy meeting – one of those little illusions (lies) many salespeople tell themselves to get through the day.

So, what now? Bob pulls out his shotgun and starts firing away, if for no other reason than for the mistaken belief that he needs to fill the silence. He certainly has not established any kind of rapport; he is just walking a couple of strangers around the building. There is really no point to what he is doing. Bob and the prospect have no shared vision. There are lots of facts, statements and features tossed about, but few if any questions, lots of talking, and little if any true listening. Bob thinks he is listening, asking questions, uncovering needs and wants.

He answers what he thinks are objections, even before he's verified whether the objections are true objections. Bob thinks he is building rapport. He thinks he's covered everything that should be covered, and he sure hope something sticks. He might even give the prospective customers a little box of chocolates at the end of their visit or, better yet, drag out his general manager for a meet and greet. These last two items (especially introducing the general manager) make Bob feel like he is being very proactive, that he is taking that extra step and outdoing his competition, but, it's an illusion. Even with a well-thought-out site visit, where needs have been fully established, the prospective customer ultimately wants to know or feel that his salesperson – not the general manager – will make it happen for them.

The chocolates, meeting the general manager, it all falls flat and rings hollow, because Bob hasn't established in his mind nor, more importantly, in the customer's mind, what the real needs are. He has not cultivated a basis for discussion. Sure, he might use the general manager and the box of chocolates as the "icing on the cake." But first, he has to bake the cake! That's where the disconnect is. The customer (whether he consciously realizes it or not) is still at step one, but Bob is at step three or four. From a tennis perspective, he took his eye off the ball. He is playing the next point – or really the next two points – instead of playing the point at hand. So, guess what? He loses the point and, in this case, probably the game, too.

So, what has really happened here with our Shotgun Salesperson? He ends up in that strange little space I call, "THINK, WISH, HOPE … Something Happens." When he goes back to his office, Bob's boss drops by and asks how it went. He says, "Oh yeah, the site went really well; I think they really liked our venue a lot. We spent 45 minutes together and we got along great." It sounds good, it sounds really good but, again, it is usually an illusion. About 24 to 48 hours later Bob will be saying to himself, "I really hope this group books. It would really help me make my goal for this quarter. If I make this booking, I'll exceed my quota and get a nice bonus."

Well, two weeks go by and Bob hasn't heard anything further from this hot prospect. He has sent two follow-up emails; one went unreturned and the other got a short response saying they were still reviewing everything. Of course, because Bob was in a rush and re-sorted to the Shotgun Sales Approach, he never really asked any "truly substantial" questions to determine the potential customer's actual needs and wants. And he never got that all-important agreement as to what the mutually agreed to, specific, "next steps" would be. It was all left kind of vague; at most, he had only agreed to send them a proposal. Other salespeople, of course, have been asking Bob about the space he has on hold and he keeps telling them (in a very professional manner) that he should know in another week. Bob's boss is no longer asking him about the event because he's forgotten about it. Of course, Bob still remembers it. He can't forget it because he has gotten himself hopelessly tied up in "hoping" this business books.

I remember a sales manager who went through this exact scenario. His fairy tale was that "it looked really good." Every week I would ask and every week I would get the same response. After three weeks, I put a little bit more pressure on the salesperson. I asked what comments the prospect had about our proposal after reviewing it. The response: The decision maker had our proposal on his desk, but he had not yet had a chance to look at it. I could see the handwriting on the wall. Too bad the sales manager couldn't. He was still hoping.

And after asking one or two more questions, I established that the "prospect" who had visited our site was not the decision maker, and the proposal was clearly not the decision maker's priority. You will find in sales, serious decision makers make the time for important things. If they don't, it is telling you something you need to know.

And so, in both examples, the salesperson finds himself saying things like, "What am I going to do if they don't book?" At this point, he has passed through that little town called "Hope" and is heading right into the suburbs of downtown "Desperationville" – a small bed-room community on the outskirts of the "City of Hopeful Losers." Not a pretty sight. The message here is very clear and very simple:

> Less is More: Less Scattered...More Precise.
>
> It's about making things happen, not hoping something happens.

If you have no detailed plan and have not done the basic research, you will always be in shotgun mode. You will always be nervous, anxious and fearful. You will always be in a rush and you will always talk too much and too quickly. Lastly, you will always come across (to the customer) as someone who does not fully know what he is talking about. You will not come across as confident and successful and, therefore, you cannot be entrusted with their business.

Are you hoping for a sale (the "Shotgun Approach") or are you making sales happen? Hope is not a strategy – never has been, never will be. If anything, it is a hopeless strategy. Don't fall victim to hope. In the pages that follow, we are going to create a new story line...a new game. We are going to keep things ridiculously simple and, most important of all, we are going to play to win.

Now, let's get started.

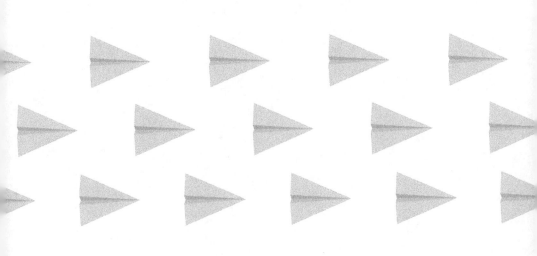

SECTION 1

THE CORE

"The greater danger, for most of us, lies not in setting our aim too high and falling short; but in setting our aim too low, and achieving our mark...."[10] *– Michelangelo*

[10] Megaessays.com

CHAPTER 1

What's the Catering and Events Sales Game All About?

Let's be honest: Based on the Shotgun Sales Approach, it is easy to see why salespeople generally do not have the best of reputations. Descriptors, such as "not informed," "not knowledgeable," "unprepared," or even "manipulative and misleading" can apply quite frequently. Bad enough the public thinks this way, but many salespeople even think this way about themselves. How many times have you heard, "Oh, he is a booking machine" or "She can schmooze anyone" or "He's a natural – he can talk you into anything." You must admit, all of these statements have an underlying negative tone. The choice of words reflects a certain callousness, coarseness, even cynicism about both salespeople and customers. The words objectify both parties. They betray a bureaucratic focus of only seeing the customer through the lens of a transaction, not a relationship. This can result in the customer feeling something was forced on them or, worse, slipped by them because the salesperson was not completely forthright. This is "the" challenge for anyone in sales, because realistically the public at large has a strong tendency to be skeptical of any salesperson until they prove themselves capable.

Unfortunately, there are quite a few relatively new and inexperienced salespeople out there (and some, too, with years of experience) who do not excel in sales, either due to lack of training, insufficient motivation, lack of understanding and/or constant job hopping. These individuals are also usually working in offices where they are surrounded by some of the same individuals I referenced in the first paragraph.

Although not cynical and coarse themselves – these less-than-stellar performers are exposed on a daily basis to this mix of negative talk, and it's not long before they fall prey to the same negative mind set.

Compounding the situation is an industry-wide tendency to rely on corporate jargon, a cavalier use of buzz words and catchy phrases, such as, "I'm going to call that prospect next week to get a pulse." This further contributes to dehumanizing and commoditizing the sales profession. This kind of shortcut language is focused on making you sound like you know what you are talking about.

It is also not uncommon to see a catering sales manager, with a big smile on his face, nervously rocking back and forth while simultaneously nodding his head in response to almost anything a customer says, all the while maintaining unbroken eye contact because he was taught to do this in sales school. It is painfully obvious he is over-eager – almost desperate – to please, whether or not he is prepared to deliver the goods. By contrast, the best salespeople – those who win and win often – keep things very simple and make it look easy. Behind the façade though is a very disciplined structure and a deep faith in the pillars – the fundamentals of great salesmanship.

It is said your thoughts drive and can change your actions. I am also a huge believer in the converse: If you change your actions, your thinking will follow. Both concepts apply in sales and indispensable performers are keenly aware of this.

PILLAR # 1--NEEDS...WANTS

The purpose of selling is, quite simply, to meet and, preferably, exceed all a customer's needs and most of his wants, while also generating profitable revenue for your company/venue. That's it. Nothing more and nothing less. It is the very reason for our existence, yet so many just don't seem to get this.

Needs? Wants? Aren't they pretty much the same? In terms of the principles of selling it all comes down to finding out exactly what a particular customer needs, what his objectives are and the purpose for each event. No matter what they say to the contrary, many salespeople make the huge mistake of thinking it's mostly about product features and price. To be in the game though, you must first fully understand a customer's needs. What are their requisites? What are their requirements, their "must haves"? For example, a prospective customer might tell you:

- We need the Grand Ballroom for the first Friday in November for our annual day-long conference with access starting at 11:00 p.m. the night before. We also need lunch for 300, along with six breakout rooms all day and all on one floor. In the main conference room, we need at least a 15-foot-high ceiling, rear-screen projection and an easily accessible adjacent area to accommodate 10 table-top exhibits.

Or:

- We need to have access to the Grand Ballroom of your facility at 2:30 p.m. to start set-up for a dinner for 600 people at round tables of 10. All seating has to be on one level with clear sight lines to a built-in stage.

In both examples, the customer has stated some very clear, very specific, very tangible needs. These are all clearly articulated needs. In the second example, they said they need to have access to the Grand Ballroom at 2:30 p.m. This raises a question: Why do they need access at 2:30 p.m.? Could they get in at 4:00 p.m. or 5:00 p.m. and still accomplish what they need for set-up purposes? You need to question that. Well, the customer says, we have a very complicated multi-screen AV presentation to set up, plus we need to do sound checks and rehearse several key presenters and awardees. That makes sense. This is clearly a need, I would say.

But what if the customer said he would like to have the additional set-up time to place all his program books and registration material, or he would like to review his slide presentation. He says he would feel more comfortable, not rushed, if he had earlier access. This sure sounds like a want, to me. After all, there are alternate means of getting those tasks accomplished without starting set up at 2:30 p.m. So, you have two completely different situations, different reasons for wanting additional set-up time. By asking a few questions, you establish what the real needs and wants are. By asking – about history in other venues, about how complicated or basic their audiovisual presentation is – you start to get the true picture of both the customer's needs and wants.

Intangible Needs

Let's look at the second example: A request for round tables of 10 for 600 with access to the ballroom starting at 2:30 p.m. What if, after a few questions, the salesperson uncovers the fact that last year, at another venue, the group before them ran 45 minutes late? This caused them to get into the ballroom late which, in turn, threw their entire event off schedule and caused a huge amount of unnecessary stress. They could not afford to have that happen again. Yes, the client outlined very clear, very specific, tangible needs. However, an even more important intangible, unspoken need was being expressed, as well. Wasn't the customer really saying, "Hey, I need some reassurance from you this will not happen to me at your venue. I need to know what your experience has been with this kind of situation. How would you address it? What steps do you currently take to prevent this from happening?" Other examples of intangible needs might be such statements as:

- We want to energize our sales force at this meeting.
- We want to showcase new products to our major vendors at this conference.
- We want an environment that is conducive to training and learning.
- We want to reward/acknowledge our top performers (or customers).
- We want to make a statement about our new (or expanding) company or organization.
- We want our wedding to make a statement about who we are.

Statements that directly or indirectly imply greater visibility or increased prestige fall into the category of intangible needs, too. In the case of a wedding or anniversary, there can be countless intangibles, ranging from wanting to be over-the-top ostentatious to simply wanting to create harmony, happiness and peace of mind for the entire family. For example, a bridal couple may want (although unmentioned) your assurance that you will keep them safe from any kind of embarrassment on their special day. In the case of a marriage involving two different cultures, your awareness and sensitivity to that, knowledge and experience in planning a menu reflective of both cultures, and coordination of the wedding itself, would all be of concern to the bridal couple and to their families. In almost all cases, intangible needs are not directly articulated by the customer. You need to sense them and draw them out. And here's food for thought:

> A customer's intangible needs almost always take precedence over their tangible needs.

The Who and What of It

So, from the very start, it's all about understanding and sensing customer needs – sorting out real needs from simple wants. Significant differences in facilities, format, even design and menu, would be dictated by the audience in attendance. You'll want to know, for example:

- Is this a meeting for employees only, or is this an event for established VIP customers?
- Is this event to attract new customers, or is this an end-of-year holiday celebration for everyone in the company?
- Is the purpose of this meeting to assist employees who are being outplaced from their jobs?
- Is this event marking the first address by the new president of this company to all employees?

- Is the company rebranding itself, and is this meeting the official launch directed at the employees? Or is the launch directed at the company's key customers?

What might both the tangible and intangible needs be in each of these scenarios? The audience and purpose of the event will dictate those needs. And those needs are critical, though their wants are not. Wants are really what we call "value adds" and are built upon needs.

> In the later stages of the sales process, the best salespeople will come back to this discussion of needs to ensure there is a definite perceived fit between what they are selling and what the customer needs.

Needs? Wants? Sorting it out all comes down to the salesperson asking the prospective customer a few logical questions.

Don't Assume

Sometimes a salesperson will "assume" what a customer's needs and wants are or, worse, what their needs will be – without even asking. Such assumptions indicate you are not really engaging this potential customer; you are on autopilot and just going through the motions. When you assume the wrong needs, you can pretty much assume you will lose the business.

Here is an email from a salesperson trying to book an event at his facility, but the customer was also strongly considering another site: a large very distinguished private club:

> *Are you familiar with the event space at XXX Venue? I am competing for an event. They are offering (prospective client) complimentary meeting space plus complimentary built-in production gear. They are also offering their roof-top terrace for the post-reception. We had originally offered*

(ZZ room) as a potential reception space, which they were not pleased with.

Here are some of the points I will highlight to them. Please let me know if there are any other ideas on how to sell against XXX Venue.

1. *In case of bad weather, it is risky to hold an event in an outside location in June.*
2. *They would most likely have to bring in a caterer that will not be to the level of our culinary team.*
3. *They will most likely not have a dedicated event manager to give them the attention that we do.*
4. *They will not offer the unique service programs that we do such as....*
5. *They may be less expensive, but there will be no comparison on the level of experience and expertise.*

Let's examine this note:

- My first reaction was if you do not know the competitor, then you are really not "competing" for this business. You might be taking your best shot, but it is a shot in the dark. The five points this sales manager outlined appear, for the most part, to be broad-based and unfounded assumptions, not confirmed needs and/or wants, nor even confirmed facts regarding the venue in question. The first question in my mind was: *Do the five points relate back to the customer's stated needs and objectives?* I suspect needs and wants were never unearthed to begin with. Therefore, I suspect that none of the five points would have any impact on the prospective customer and may have actually come across negatively, further turning the prospect off from seriously considering the venue.

- Why not just call the person you are seeking advice from on this matter? It would certainly allow for a much more direct and candid conversation regarding the issues, plus save time. It has been my experience that the more a salesperson does not speak directly, the more he seems to opt for putting together detailed emails. This can very easily lead you into that trap I have referred to as the "illusion of selling."

- As far as "complimentary built in production gear" goes, most hotel venues will sometimes reduce or, on occasion, even waive room rental, but a hotel venue would never waive audiovisual production fees; hotel business models are simply not set up that way. So, was the hotel even in the running to begin with for this event when the competition was offering to waive 35% or more of the total overall charges, plus waive the very profitable component of room rental, too? And second, was this even an attractive piece of business for the hotel? Did it meet their needs and criteria as a venue?

- In terms of it being risky to host an event outdoors in June well, it had become a very popular option. I also suspected the venue probably had a back-up plan in case of rain. So, I didn't quite get the "fear factor" thing going on here. None of this would have helped bring the customer closer to the salesperson. In fact, it would distance the salesperson from the customer and draw his motives into question. The message to the customer would be: "You are wrong."

- In points two and three, the salesperson (in saying "most likely") leaves himself open to the possibility that the venue in question will, in fact, do everything in house without having to bring in an outside caterer. And, even if they did, there are many outstanding outside caterers. So why go down that road? It's a non-starter. A good lawyer will tell you not to pose a question you don't already know the answer to. The same applies here.

- And in points four and five, the salesperson offers no proof and/or references to similar organizations they have served to support his position. In total, the salesperson has, by inference, made decisions and come to conclusions as to what the customer's needs "should" be, not what they are.

- Finally, all the points this salesperson would "remind them of" would be conjecture and thus come across negatively. There is mention of risk in the first point, the word "not" is used in three other points, and the last point implies "not." Wouldn't he have wanted to couch his responses to this potential customer in language that reflects his (and the venue's) ability to better fulfill their needs?

If I were this salesperson, I would have checked the competitor's website and/or walked over to the venue to see it for myself. Then I would have gotten on the phone and really probed this prospective customer as to what he considered to be his two or three most important needs. I would think the major issue was the customer's need for exclusivity and the ambiance of the other facility. The venue in question was not in the hotel's traditional competitive set; it was a very distinguished private club located in a very wealthy area of the city. In addition, there is a significant price differential between major hotels and private clubs. Quite frankly, I would say the customer was probably working on the premise that the club was the better and preferred option. Perhaps knowing the square footage of the conference facilities at the club would have been helpful. Possibly the club overstated their capacity, which in turn would raise a question as to their capabilities. If they did overstate – and by a significant margin – a compelling case could be made, using a square-footage comparison.

Here is a very similar example:

> *The XX Organization are leaning toward going back to xxx venue, located on the water. Besides the fact it is*

*difficult to get transportation to and from this venue and the
fact our ballroom is grander, do you have a few suggestions
on how to sell against them?*

My answer was no, I do not have any ideas as to how to sell against them. I do have some thoughts as to how to potentially draw your prospective customer toward us, though. I always think implicit in the term "selling against" is a decision to stop listening and stop looking for needs/wants. This decision further directs inexperienced salespeople to start blurting out all their reasons why the potential customer should book their venue. The salesperson in this example is also making the classic mistake of trying to sell features, not benefits based on real needs. All his efforts only contribute to developing a potentially contentious atmosphere, because the focus is on "selling against" (negative) versus helping the customer "open up to" (positive). The attitude coming through in this note is all about what I, the salesperson, want and need, not about what the customer wants and needs.

Regrettably (though I don't think the salesperson was consciously doing this), the emphasis was on "telling" the customer he should book here and pointing out what's wrong with the venue he has been using for eight years. There was no uncovering of the customer's needs.

The transportation issue? Since the event has been at the same venue for eight years, I think this is a non-issue. Further compounding this, the event is on a Saturday when transportation is much easier around the city, versus mid-week.

Perhaps the organization is outgrowing the facility? Perhaps there have been service or food issues? Perhaps there is new leadership involved and they want to change it up and take the event to another level? It appears these and similar questions were never asked.

"Our Ballroom is grander"? Okay, what exactly is our "grander ballroom" going to do for this customer? Or, more likely (since the event has been in the same venue for eight years), the customer couldn't care less about "grand." Who knows?

"The Blah, Blah, Blah" Needs

Another approach many salespeople take is making broad general statements as to the needs of the customer, such as they need a smooth-running event, VIP treatment or "The Wow Factor." What does all that mean? Absolutely nothing. It's all too vague and an indication the salesperson has not listened to, nor questioned, the potential customer thoroughly, has not done his homework. And, as far as "The Wow Factor" goes, it tends to be more hype than anything else. At best, "Wow Factors" are the icing on the cake. Most customers want what you promise ("the cake"), not necessarily any more and certainly not less. Again, it is not that complicated. Needs-based questions are designed to elicit where the customer is trying to go. They are future directed.

The Real Needs

Customers' needs can run the gamut from a more exciting and creative menu to improved or quicker service from both the salesperson and the venue's operational staff. The customer may need a larger or smaller facility. Maybe they want a more centrally located venue that is closer and more easily accessible to transportation. Maybe they want to get their costs under control – have a more reasonable price point or conserve or reduce costs. It could be the customer is more focused on the operational side of the event and is looking to streamline what in the past has been a complicated process. Their need could be to have a smooth, flawless flow to the event. Perhaps the organization is going through a change and wants a new facility that better reflects a certain new image they have of their organization. They may be looking for "name "recognition. Or, maybe they just want to work with a more experienced salesperson and banquet staff that is more flexible, e.g. they allow for changes, offer more choice of entrees or are simply willing to help when the customer says I need a favor, instead of saying, "Well the policy is…." Most customer needs will, for the most part, revolve around these elements:

1. Menu	4. Facilities	7. Location
2. Service	5. Operations	8. Flexibility
3. Image	6. Cost Control	9. Customer Advocate

We are all familiar with the expression "Getting back to basics." If you stick with the basics to begin with, you never need to get back to them. In real estate, it's all about "location, location, location." In sales it's all about "needs, needs, needs." It's not complicated.

PILLAR #2: LISTEN...THEN QUESTION

The very best salespeople meet all the needs and most of the wants of their customers. The way they go about this is, again, very simple: they *listen first* and *question second*. The very first step in selling is: Active-Focused Listening – being fully engaged with the customer, fully present, and fully in the moment. Good questions follow logically from active listening: Ask well thought-out, logically planned questions in an order that will naturally uncover real needs and wants – the real hot buttons.

Active-Focused Listening is a skill that must be developed; most of us are not born with it. Hearing is only paying attention to the words. Active listening is paying attention to everything, including the emotions and feelings. This kind of listening helps you understand the customer's desires, expectations and thought process. It is essential to ensuring that the interaction stays positive and contributes to building trust.

Active-Focused Listening to the customer has several similarities to tennis:

> Keep your head up and focused on the ball until after you hit through. Focus only on the ball from the moment your opponent picks up the ball to serve until the very end of the match. Stay physically relaxed and calm. Do not allow doubt, fear or over-thinking to enter your mind, otherwise you'll blow the shot. You don't think, you just play. You don't force anything, you just watch and play. In other words, you don't get ahead of yourself.

Similarly, in sales, your focus must be almost 100% on that customer, on his words, on his inflection, on his body language, on his facial expression. The focus is on him, not on you. Your questions have to sound natural, and they will if you focus on the customer.

STAYING IN THE NOW

Too often – we have all done this – we jump ahead of ourselves and our customers. Instead of keeping our heads up (staying "in the moment") and focusing on the ball (listening), we start telling the prospective customer all the wonderful things we can do for them and/or reciting a litany of features that have no (or only partial) bearing on their real needs. We succumb to talking away about ourselves and our venue, instead of simply listening.

How is this reflected on the "playing field"? Unconsciously what happens is the salesperson's head shifts down to look at all his diagrams, brochures and fact sheets – you know, all the stuff he wants to talk about. In so doing, the salesperson breaks his focus, takes his eye off the ball. He is not fully listening to his prospective customer. The customer may be trying to provide him with invaluable information, yet the salesperson's mind has raced ahead to where he thinks the customer is headed. The salesperson may be jumping to the wrong conclusion, but even if jumping to the right conclusion, he still misses key details. Prospects and customers alike will tell you what you need to do to sell to them if you simply shut up and listen. Likewise, you are not listening if at the same time you are mentally preparing your response, and too many do just that. They jump in while the customer is speaking because they think they understand the customer's problem or issue. However, if you are giving your immediate advice, in most cases the advice is premature and perhaps even unwelcome. Aim to listen and question to understand, not necessarily to reply.

Management guru Peter Drucker has said, "The most important thing in communication is hearing what isn't said." [11] Most salespeople listen selectively, particularly when it comes to objections. Too much

---

[11] keithwebb.com

talk leads to too many missed opportunities to "hear" buying signals. When you are so busy talking, you miss the opportunities to watch and listen for those slight shades of difference in speech, tone and body language that indicate the customer is moving toward you or drawing back from you. If you are relaxed, have a clear mind, slow down and are focused on the other person, you can actually see and feel this non-verbal dynamic play out. It is very subtle. If you talk too much, I guarantee you will miss the signals. If you really want to "Wow" a customer – wow him with your listening skills.

New salespeople tend to talk too much and too quickly. A certain amount of this is due to nerves and inexperience. Lack of preparation and thinking they must do most of the talking are contributing factors, as well. They either talk too much about their products (to show off their knowledge) or they ask one question after another – in a rapid-fire manner – as if they are running down a checklist. Staying calm and simply listening first helps you improve your ability to listen effectively. Second, if you do, you have a much better chance of communicating back more constructively when you do speak. In the same vein, by listening, you leave yourself open to more options.

Going on "Autopilot"

Some salespeople will walk into a meeting with potential customers and immediately start interacting with them without having given much, if any, prior thought. The salesperson starts talking and doing the same things he did yesterday when meeting with another prospective customer, and maybe that person did book. However, every potential customer is different.

> What worked for me last Saturday in my weekly tennis match will not necessarily work this week. This week's match will be slightly, to possibly completely, different from last week's match, based on several variables that I have to be open to observing.

What usually happens is we find ourselves talking with a new prospect today but replaying what we talked about with another prospect yesterday. Whatever we are doing just doesn't seem to be working; we don't seem to be connecting with this person. We are caught off guard and in the pressure of the moment; we "do more" of what we did yesterday. What we should be doing is slowing down...recalibrating. Just like in tennis.

> When in trouble, slow down and calm yourself.
> Concentrate on intentionally slowing your breathing
> and movement so you can "open yourself up" - however
> unconsciously - to what is actually happening right now.

As noted, many salespeople make the mistake of sitting down with a prospective customer and very shortly thereafter start reviewing diagrams, brochures, iPad photos, etc. This is nothing more than a crutch for the salesperson. Untrained salespeople start with these props. Is there a place for the diagrams, photos, etc.? Absolutely, but not at this early juncture. The brochures and floor plans will not do the job of simply listening and talking with a customer.

The main characteristic of an unsuccessful sales conversation is that the salesperson is doing most of the talking. When you are talking, you are not learning anything. In the end, if you are the one doing all the talking, you are creating stress, tension and usually resistance in the customer's mind. Good salespeople are calm and open. The conversation is conducted in a relaxed/fluid manner, which spurs open dialogue.

TALKING YOURSELF OUT OF A SALE

Here is an example of something that could have been handled quite differently. A national sales manager was trying to secure a major convention and I was assisting him in that effort. The event involved a very large number of overnight guest rooms and a huge amount of catering.

We arranged to have a private luncheon for all key decision makers in one of our VIP board rooms. We agreed that, following lunch, we would conduct a tour of our facilities. To facilitate that, we prepared a PowerPoint presentation with diagrams of the two major ballrooms they would require for their event. The thought was to review these diagrams with them after lunch and just prior to our tour. It would help establish a visual in our prospective customers' minds just before we embarked upon our tour.

Shortly after we all sat down to lunch, and following all the usual introductions, I expected we would all settle into a leisurely meal, during which we would get comfortable with our potential customers, get to know them a little better, and start to do some further probing for needs and wants. We would listen a lot and do a lot more follow-up questioning, if the flow of our conversation allowed for it. In other words, we would start with where the customer was and move on from there.

Anyway, within a few minutes my partner proceeded to go on a "Data Dump." Besides not making any real eye contact with our guests, there was also next to no listening nor questioning of our potential customers. There was no focus on – nor probing for – what their needs and wants might be. I was shocked. At one point (when it looked like the sales manager was momentarily pausing to take in more oxygen), I interjected that we were first of all delighted to have all of them with us today and we very much appreciated their taking time out of their busy schedules to come in and review our facilities. Continuing on, I said we would be very interested in hearing from them about their experience in the past, and if there was anything they were looking to do differently or to change in the future. I made it a point to maintain good eye contact with each person at the table. I was inviting responses.

At that point, one of our guests started to discuss in pretty specific detail how they had 400 attendees for their conference last year but had to turn away over 150 additional people because the ballroom could only accommodate up to 400. She said they would like to be able to accommodate up to 650 guests next year, plus they needed five break-out meeting rooms. This guest's wonderful needs-based comments were interrupted by my partner, who jumped in to continue his data dump – important things, such as the total number of overnight rooms at our venue and how many awards we had won. He forgot it's not about us, it's about them, particularly right now. He had stopped listening.

Following our luncheon and prior to our tour, my partner and I presented our PowerPoint of the two major ballrooms. Again, my partner felt compelled to jump right in and start talking about one of the ballrooms being 27,000 square feet, divisible into 16 sections blah… blah… blah. I could tell this had absolutely no impact on anyone, and we were about to lose a golden opportunity. I stepped forward, looking right at the woman who had talked about their attendance being 400 last year. I said, "Beverly, you mentioned earlier you would like to grow next year's conference participation to 650 guests." I paused and she nodded in agreement. I then used a laser pointer and showed her on the diagram (versus telling her) the meeting space where her 650 guests would meet. I also showed her where all her break-out meetings would be and noted that all would be on the same floor – a need she had articulated. I then proceeded to tell her about a few value-adds which I suspected might tie into a few of her as yet not fully articulated needs and wants. I mentioned, for example, that the foyer area was very large and allowed for plenty of space to conduct both registration and all coffee breaks simultaneously. I further noted they would have this entire floor to themselves; no other event would be on the floor.

Had I been in singular control of the meeting, I might have forestalled this kind of show and tell till later, but I tried to make the best of the situation we were in – make lemonade out of lemons, so to speak. I maintained relaxed eye contact with her and everyone else on the tour. All the while, my facial and body language indicated I was open and wanted to hear feedback and questions from them. And all the while, I watched for and received confirmation they knew what I was saying, that it made sense to them, and that they saw this as fulfilling a need.

Listening is, of course, more involved than just keeping quiet and maintaining eye contact. Active-Focused Listening will naturally lead to logical and insightful follow-up questions. Even when they say they are listening, many salespeople are just waiting to come right back with their response or other pre-conceived questions and comments on their checklists. They have it backwards – it all flows from what you just heard.

LISTENING KEYS

You must "show" you are intent on understanding what you hear, as well as retaining what you have just heard. How do you do that? Here are some "Listening Keys" that will greatly help in that effort:

- 75% of the time you should be listening, 25% talking.
- Use body language. Nod and say, "Tell me more about that," or "Interesting…I never thought of that." An encouraging demeanor elicits better conversation.
- Use such phrases as, "Can you explain, or can you describe to me a bit more about the people who will be attending?"
- Say, "How can we make sure your meeting is successful?
- Say, "I can see you had several problems with last year's event." This encourages the person to talk more and reveal more which, in turn, helps you learn more.
- Ask clarifying questions to sharpen the focus of the conversation.
- Paraphrase what you think the person said and ask if you are on target.
- Take note of the person's body language and facial expressions as sources of meaning and then adapt to them.
- Make eye contact. Besides keeping your mind from wandering, it shows you are focused on the customer. Looking anywhere but at your prospect while he is speaking tells him he does not have your complete attention.
- Repeat important points the potential customer raises.
- Pause to reflect or draw out more information.
- Take notes. It shows you are genuinely interested and serious about learning more about your customer.
- Empathize by saying such things as, "I would have the same reaction as you."

- Use fewer words in your own responses (round out/complete points with crisp language). You will facilitate rapport and show you are truly listening.
- Moderate your voice tempo and adjust to the customer's tempo and pace – is his faster or slower? You will show you are tuned into him.
- Look for areas where you and the prospect agree to serve the bigger purpose of building a conversation flow and tempo that is both positive and affirmative.
- Maintain an attentive posture when you ask questions. It indicates you are truly engaged and interested in listening to his responses.
- Use open-ended questions once you have established a basic rapport. It further encourages customers to open up about their feelings and motivations.
- Hold off on educating or explaining too early in the conversation. You will miss opportunities for the prospective customer to open up.

By activating these verbal and non-verbal techniques, and employing mostly open- ended/relative questions, you will gain the most important information. Intersperse a few closed-end questions, as well (such as: How many people will you have? What time does the event start? What kind of set up – classroom or theatre? Will you have any coffee breaks? Will you have a sit-down or buffet lunch?), but don't make these questions the focus of your interaction. Ineffective salespeople ask closed-end questions almost exclusively, and almost always too early in the conversation. This creates tension and impatience and reduces their customer interactions to cold-hearted transactions. The customer is thinking, "What's with all the questions? I just need to know the price!" And so, you are back to the old dates, rates, space scenario that dominates the catering scene. In Chapter 8 we will delve much further into how to listen to and question a potential customer most effectively.

So, listen and observe before you talk. And when you do talk, lead with mostly open-ended questions. Be natural and spontaneous and avoid the poor salesperson's habit of talking too much about your company or facility. At this point, you are building rapport, not selling a product. Keep it overwhelmingly about your prospect and you will naturally find points in the conversation to interject information about what you can offer.

> The professional salesperson does not want to project an image of being a "know it all." Just the opposite; he always demonstrates that he wants to learn more.

PILLAR # 3: LIKE VS. TRUST

Why do people buy? Why do they buy from you and not from me? The single most important factor is: Do I trust you? Do I trust you to deliver on your promises? To quote the great legendary salesman Zig Ziglar:

"If people like you they will listen to you, but if they trust you they will do business with you."[12]

Ziglar went on to say that integrity is the most important persuasion tool you have in your entire arsenal. It is the essence of sales, but it is deceptively simple. It's so simple we forget it, overlook it or discount it. We think sales just has to be more complicated than that. We think we have to build a case with facts and figures, as well as product statements and features (The Kiss of Death!).

ARE YOU AUTHENTIC?

As you engage a prospective customer, he is starting to get a sense of exactly who you are, and this is way before you get to presenting solutions.

---

[12] Rohandredge.com

A perception starts to come together quickly as to whether you are real, sincere – yes likeable – but more important: Authentic.

Trust starts with "authenticity." The world is literally starving for authentic people. When you think about it, don't we all want people, or at least someone, somewhere, to be what they appear to be? Ask yourself: Are you authentic in everything you say and do with your customers?

Authentic people tend to be the "what you see is what you get" kind of people. They also have a very much "you get what you give" approach to life. You can sense it almost immediately upon meeting them. In other words, they are comfortable with who they are. They are fully present. They are not looking through notes or checking their watches while a customer is talking to them. They speak in every day understandable language, not corporate sound bites. They keep all those little promises – call when they say they will and address issues quickly and completely. They are very candid, and have no trouble saying, "You know, I could be wrong on that," if the situation warrants. If there is a concern or disagreement, they put it right on the table for discussion. And, if they do not meet an expectation, they own up to it right away, apologize, and learn from their mistakes. All these actions reinforce their authenticity and therefore their trustworthiness. In the later phases of a sale, this will help your customer believe that your advice, suggestions and explanations are valid and well-meaning. Your ability to listen and question lays the important groundwork in this effort. Your ability to stay in the now is an equally contributing factor to establishing yourself as genuine.

ARE YOU A PROMISE MAKER?

In the long term, you only earn trust by demonstrating it. People must see it in action, you can't just talk about it. Too often – well-intentioned as they may be – salespeople get caught up in the moment and over commit. They promise that the facility will execute something they are physically incapable of delivering. Granted, this does not always result in losing a sale, but it does not add to building trust either. As a promise maker, you must ensure there is no discrepancy between what you promise and what you deliver. This also includes how you solve all those day-to-day issues/problems that always come about when putting together any event. This is what drives trust. Trust builds loyalty and loyalty builds repeat business and referrals.

We have all experienced the salesperson who comes across as hesitant, even to the point of being non-committal. The prospective customer immediately picks up on this as a cause for concern. After all is said and done, the customer considers the salesperson – not the company they represent – to be the number one "promise maker." Companies cannot make promises, only salespeople can.

To my point, in a recent *Investor's Business Daily* survey, over 95% of respondents placed trust first when selecting a financial adviser.[13] Trustworthiness even outweighed performance. A similar *IBD* survey in 2013 uncovered that 8.7% of investors fired their financial advisers because of trust-related problems. [14]

> As much as possible, under promise and over deliver.

Are You Customer-Focused or Venue-Focused?

In many large hotels and some standalone catering facilities, the catering sales process is separate from the event/detailing process. In other words, the salesperson sells the event to a customer and then (once the contract is signed) "turns it over" to an event manager who does all the detailing of the event and handles all the day-to-day issues with the customer from that point on. For every piece of business booked, there is a "turnover sheet," attached to the signed contract. During the transition, the event manager and sales manager meet to thoroughly review the event. The turnover sheet contains several bullet points for

---

[13] *Investor's Business Daily Special Report: Financial Advisors' Guide*, November 3, 2010.
[14] *Investor's Business Daily* survey, 2013.

the benefit of the event manager. Inexperienced event managers often resort to relying exclusively on the "turnover sheet" (which, in itself, is a very useful and constructive document, but will never give you the complete picture), rather than actively engaging with both the customer and the salesperson. Here is an example that was shared with me:

- A salesperson arranged a small cocktail party for 250 guests. The client needed a very basic reception package for two hours. He also mentioned (but he did not put it in his notes) they would be giving out a few awards. The salesperson reviewed the event and these points with the assigned event manager. He was on a business trip on the day of the event, but upon his return asked how it went. He was told all went well but they did have to scramble for a microphone and podium at the last minute for a few speeches and awards. What was apparent was almost all "communication" was by email; it was all transactional. The service failure started with the salesperson and was carried over into the event manager's interactions with the client. A brief conversation with the client somewhere along the way could have prevented the error.

The overwhelming message here for a salesperson is to make sure your turn-over notes are correct and very detailed. It is so important that event managers have the proper information before interacting with the client. The more communication between the salesperson and the event manager, the better the experience for the guest.

- On another occasion, a long-standing annual customer asked me about the FedEx charges that were never on his bill for prior events. When I questioned the event manager, he said the client signed off on it in the event orders. My question though was, "Was it discussed?" Ultimately, the answer to that question was "No." As it turns out, the event manager did not want to take the charge off the bill because his boss would be upset with him. I wanted to take the charge off the bill because it was the right thing to do for our customer. My emphasis was on the relationship, on preserving trust. The customer called me because he sensed he needed someone to fight the internal corporate bureaucracy he was being unintentionally subjected to by the event manager. He was turning to the person he knew would be his customer advocate in this matter and would bend over backwards to address the unstated need for someone to simply do the right thing.

Great salespeople know how to challenge the system when a standard isn't good enough or is neither working in the customer's – nor the venue's – best interest. In a corporate structure this can tend to not go over well at first, since companies ask for consistency and conformity. However, at the same time, great companies always reward and promote innovators.

> Employ the golden rule: Treat others as you would like to be treated.

Turn Over the Event – Not the Relationship

When a catering salesperson turns an event over to an event manager, he may be turning over the event, but not the customer relationship. There should never be a separation between the salesperson and the event manager. It's not "my event," or "your event," it's "our event." This can be a complex juggling act, fraught with ego, seniority and other internal political issues, but if everyone involved thinks of the customer first, these issues tend to fall by the wayside. Simply referring to the event team as "we" goes a long way in this effort. In addition, if the entire team is in sync and informed every step of the way, there will be few if any surprises and/or lack of communication to hinder the customer's experience or our long-term relationship with him.

"Imagine this….

A very loyal customer's organization was hosting their 100thanniversary dinner. The problem: An insufficient lighting wash on a two-tier dais on stage. The audiovisual manager assigned to the event never called the customer to review this year's event. He simply copied the same arrangements from last year's dinner. But last year's dinner was held in a much smaller ballroom with a much lower ceiling and a smaller one-tier dais. This year, simple logic dictated additional lighting.

As a result of poor internal communication, the dais was mostly in the dark and each guest speaking from the podium had to say, "I know you can't see me, but I hope you can hear me." It was painful. Who was responsible?

- The audiovisual manager was clearly the person most responsible for the service failure.
- The event manager was most responsible for not noticing the issue ahead of time.
- The sales manager was equally at fault. He broke his promise to deliver the customer an outstanding event.
- The sales manager wanted to blame the banquet floor captain (and, to a degree, rightfully so) for not noticing the issue earlier in the set-up.

The sales manager, however, should have had a broader vision than either the banquet captain or the event manager. What's more, he had roughly two hours (before doors opened) to notice the issue. The manager spent the next 24 hours gathering details as to what happened and when, and who was responsible internally. The final score on this fiasco was that the other managers "learned something moving forward" (corporate speak), and the sales manager lost quite a bit of credibility and that fragile quality – "trust" (real speak) – with the customer. What the sales manager could have done was to immediately call the customer and apologize profusely for letting him down on such an important occasion; in other words, step up to the plate, stand there and listen to their customer justifiably vent. If you are ever going to have a chance to recover this relationship you have to stand there and take the heat – no matter what. This focus on having "all the details" before calling does zero to help with regaining trust – just the opposite.

The morale: Strong salespeople are very service-oriented. They take pride in their ownership of an account and make certain the service is delivered as promised. While there usually are several other individuals assigned to serve the client, the most successful salespeople are likely double-checking the key details, but not to micromanage or second guess the rest of the team. The customer, in turn, not only notices it, but it causes his trust to continue to grow. And, as I've said, trust leads to loyalty and loyalty leads to repeat bookings and referrals.

THE "LIKE ME" FOCUS

Many salespeople (and event managers and banquet floor captains), and especially new/inexperienced salespeople think, "Oh, I have to get them to like me." They put all their focus on getting people to like them, not getting people to trust them. They opt to become entertainers versus skilled professionals. And where do all these individuals get this idea? From other ineffective or inexperienced salespeople who act exactly in this fashion. Instead of focusing on needs and wants, they focus on like and fun. They may get to like and even fun, but they don't get to trust. And that's not good enough. Getting people to like you will only get you so far. If "like" is all you bring to the game, well, people see through that pretty quickly. In most cases, they will not say anything directly, but they're thinking it. Of course, you want to be likeable. But, ultimately, the more trust a customer has in you as a salesperson, the much less likely they are to be swayed by your competitors.

To my point, when hosting a major luncheon for a very prestigious organization within the financial industry I noticed the event manager and banquet floor captain were immersed in conversation all morning with the organization's on-site event coordinator. They were, as they put it, "focusing on the customer and building their relationship." Every minor request or question the coordinator had was immediately addressed because our team was "focused" on getting an excellent guest satisfaction score on the survey we sent to every customer following their event. Although securing an excellent guest satisfaction score is a very important focus, it is primarily based on fulfilling the customer's (the person who signs the contract) major needs and wants, not necessarily on all the little last minute ancillary – as well as minor – requests that can come up during the course of the event through the organization's on-site coordinator (who does not sign contracts).

Now, the on-site coordinator was closer in age to our two team members, so they naturally had a good comfort level with her. However, the real client – the president – was much older and more reserved, and no one was paying much attention to her. Following the luncheon, I spoke with the president and was informed that the luncheon food for the dais was cold and they were served last (not first, as is customary). Second, during the keynote speech, the dais guests heard quite a bit of noise (waiters talking) coming from the back of the house.

When informed of the president's critique, the two managers said, "Got it. Next time we will nail the execution of this." Well, sometimes when you cannot execute on some of the most basic and rudimentary aspects of proper service there is no next time. The real point in all of this is allowing yourself to get caught up in 1,000 little extraneous details, only to end up blowing the three most important details, is a non-starter. Oh, and by the way, the somewhat junior event coordinator left the organization six months later, but the president is still there.

The "Trust Me" Focus

In contrast, for many years I solicited a Japanese organization that hosted a major annual dinner in New York. Normally, they would not use our facility for this event. They preferred an Eastside location and a more prestigious name. I still solicited their business for 17 years and, finally, did luck out. (Everyone counts on some luck!) As it turned out, all the prestigious locations that could accommodate them were booked. Ours was one of two facilities that could accommodate their 500 guests on the preferred date.

I met with the prospective client for an in-depth discussion and review of our facilities. I put forth a proposal shortly thereafter and we quickly secured the business. When presenting me with the signed contract, the client said that for all 17 years of our interaction, she had been so impressed with my sincerity, my honesty, my follow-through and my gentle persistence. She further told me (based on her meeting, negotiations, site tour with me and my detailed and thorough proposal) she trusted me, and trusted that her event would take place exactly the way we discussed. WOW! It was one of those days where I say to myself, "…and they actually pay me to do this job!" If a comment like that from a customer doesn't make you feel pumped, then it's time for you to get out of the business.

Here's an interesting side note about this event that goes to the points of trust, knowledge, honesty and being a promise maker. For our first course, it was agreed we would have both a fork and chopsticks at each place setting. I had specifically asked for, and put in writing, a request for chopsticks to be of an upgraded quality and individually wrapped in a simple white wrapper without any inscription. During the set-up for the event our client was immersed in the production/ rehearsing speakers, etc., and did not notice what I started to notice: The wrapper was not white and featured Mandarin lettering. This was a Japanese event, not a Chinese event! A small error you might say? Not if you know anything about the history between these two countries. There is a deep underlying tension between the two going back to World War II. This could have been a monumental and extremely embarrassing mistake.

Besides being absolutely incorrect and unacceptable, this showed a real lack of understanding, sensitivity and detail orientation. I made our client aware of the situation right away and apologized for the error on our part. She was very comfortable going with only the forks and we quickly made the adjustment. The issue of the chopsticks themselves was easy to correct. The more important issue is what if we hadn't caught it before the guests entered the ballroom? Although an embarrassing situation for us, it would be beyond embarrassing and, in fact, devastating for our client. The client was deeply relieved we caught the error in time, and that we were aware enough of her needs (in this case her unspoken need) to step in and address it quickly.

In the examples outlined thus far (think of a doctor, lawyer or a financial consultant), isn't "trust" the more important issue? Isn't "like" secondary? In the case of the chopsticks, in one sense the chopsticks were not the issue. It was more a matter of what effect this near-blunder could have on the customer's trust level.

Another incredibly important ("must have") component to this concept of trust is the ability to empathize with your customer, as clearly illustrated in the last example. As a matter of fact, if you do not have empathy for your customer you have absolutely no chance of ever developing trust. You must be able to put yourself in your customer/prospect's shoes, see things from his perspective. The best salespeople can sense whatever their customers are feeling and modify their approach and pace almost immediately (and intuitively), based on any given situation or customer reaction. In turn, customers sense the salesperson understands, is aware, is sensitive to and can relate to their experiences, feelings and thoughts. For empathetic salespeople, the word "schmoozer" doesn't exist in their vocabulary.

Don't confuse empathy with sympathy. "Sympathy" is looking at a situation from the outside in and feeling sorry for someone. "Empathy" is the ability to put yourself in that person's place and sense how he is feeling, how a particular situation is impacting him right now. Regarding empathetic salespeople, you will hear customers say things like, "He gets it," or "We are on the same wavelength," or "He did the right thing," or "He understands what I am looking for." That's empathy. The best salespeople are not confined to some preconceived sales presentation, but can function in real-time customer interactions. They key into customers and go beyond what other salespeople do. The empathetic salesperson will quickly apologize when their venue makes a mistake, and will go about correcting it immediately, instead of going on defense and trying to rationalize the error away. Too many fall into the bad habit of thinking and acting totally from a venue perspective. You have to do both.

Great salespeople know you must treat people as you would want to be treated. They also bring a sense of urgency and immediacy to all they say and do. This, in turn, furthers the perception they are honest, transparent (no hidden agendas) and know what they are talking about.

When you have authenticity, you have trust, and when you have trust you have successfully established your authority.

Integrity is everything. You either have it or you don't. It doesn't take too much to lose a customer. However, if you demonstrate you have integrity, most customers will be much more likely to at least give you the opportunity to correct the problem and redeem yourself on a future event. This is because deep down, they trust you.

Trust Busters

Some other contributing disconnects to trust that lead to negative results are:

- Sales managers who are not available nor accessible leading up to and/or on the day of the event. If possible, the sales manager should also make it a point to be visible to both the client and the banquet managers handling the execution of the event. He should also be appropriately and professionally dressed for the occasion.

- Sales managers who repeatedly say to customers: "Got it" or "Perfect." English translation: "Okay, I got the gist of what you are saying, and I want to move on. I'm busy, can't you tell?"

- Saying "No problem." What's wrong with "You're welcome"? "No problem" is unintentionally condescending, whereas "Your welcome" is more positive, more of an invitation.

- Often when there is a service failure, we hear too much about how and why it happened and not enough about what we are doing and will continue to do to lessen the effect on the customer.

- The more "I" and "My" you use in your verbal and written communications with customers, the more you alienate them. People start to sense this is all about you, not them. The best salespeople say "We" and "Our" far more frequently.

So, you are the chief promise-maker in this whole business of catering sales. The operating departments are promise-keepers. We need the support of all those operating departments. But, to the customer, you are the face of the company. That's why salespeople have the greatest burden of trust. They have the most to win and the most to lose.

Event management is a fairly new development in the catering field. Most event managers have one to three years' experience; event managers with five to seven-plus years of experience are the exception, not the norm. That type of lengthy experience, though, is invaluable to both your and your customer's success. We will continue to struggle with this as event management evolves. Having said that though, I still do fully support the idea of turning events over to an event management team. Overall, there can potentially be many more pluses than minuses with this process, but it must be navigated carefully by all parties.

Pillar # 4—Fear...to...Belief...to Winning

I recently read an article that noted sales jobs are always plentiful because so many people are afraid of the job. You don't hear much if anything about fear, however, in any sales training course. Yet, fear is acknowledged by all good salespeople, while it is denied (to their detriment) by most poorly trained salespeople. Synonyms for fear are anxiety, doubt, panic, timidity, worry, unease and aversion. Think about that for a minute. Have any of those words ever applied to you? I suspect we all must admit "Yes" for some (occasionally), and for others, all too often. Fear creates illusions, it creates complications. Belief, on the other hand, creates clarity and focused simplicity.

Underlying absolutely everything a salesperson does or does not do is fear and its direct opposite: Belief, and the will to win. The best salespeople know, on a profoundly deep and personal level, that fear of failure creates failure. They know that to win, they must take risks. Due to this mindset, the "best of the best" adapt and change much more quickly than all the rest. To the question: "Is the customer's date flexible?" the ineffective salesperson's response is, "Well, that's the date they asked for." To the next question: "Have you spoken to the decision maker/key influencer?" they invariably respond, "No, I am dealing with the coordinator." To the next question: "Have you spoken with the coordinator? they say, "Yes, by email." All these responses indicate a lack of honesty – primarily with themselves – and, of course, fear.

When you offer up ideas, suggestions or directives for success to some salespeople, their response is the usual qualifying "Yes but…" or "What if…?" They go on to tell you all the reasons your idea will not work here, or it doesn't work in this market, or we tried that once and it failed – all the usual fear qualifiers to justify saying no.

Salespeople who are filled with "Think, Wish, Hope" (translation: self-doubt and fear) seem to do an awful lot of rationalizing. If they lose a piece of business, they don't take the time to honestly evaluate what they did and did not do correctly. They don't confront themselves. Real hope in sales begins with first being honest with yourself, and then being honest about everything you say and do related to a sale.

In sales, the root cause of fear will always be lack of honesty with ourselves, and it comes in many disguises, pride being the most prevalent. Pride makes you stop asking questions that could lead to change, because you are afraid you will look stupid. Pride puts all the focus on outward appearances. It makes you stay in your comfort zone and not challenge yourself. It makes you afraid to say you don't know what you don't know. Salespeople of this caliber also tend to resort to using much more sales jargon than do stronger performers. Most of these individuals will reluctantly admit their focus is predominately on not failing. They do not confront their fears, nor do they want to. This kind of thinking terminates any kind of thinking that includes risk. You can't think this way in sports, nor can you allow yourself to think this way in sales. Former New York Giants coach Bill Parcells used to tell his quarterback Phil Simms:

"If you are not throwing at least two interceptions today, you're not taking enough chances. I want you to be daring."[15]

---

[15] *New York Post* –Steve Serby—July 30,2013 and USA Today –Jim Corbett---August 21,2013

Fran Tarkenton, another great New York Giants quarterback, has said:

"Fear causes people to draw back from situations. It brings on mediocrity, it dulls creativity, it sets one up to be a loser in life." [16]

At best, fear generates average performance and it all but eliminates any creativity. It makes you pull back at the very moment you need to step up. Fear creates inaction, which results in risks not taken and experiences not had, and this furthers even more self-doubt and fear. The message in both quotes is clear: You need to be bold and daring. You can only do that if you overcome fear.

In tennis, when fear enters the game…

> …we say the player is "tightening up." He is becoming hesitant…second guessing his shots. He is playing tight and scared. His shots are a little bit off, a little tentative. The footwork is a bit awkward, not natural and flowing. The player is overthinking his shots, trying too hard. And, as the pressure increases, performance decreases.

When belief enters the game…

> …is the player tense and anxious? No. More than likely, his strokes are almost effortless. It flows. He has a strong, relaxed presence on the tennis court; his serve is relaxed and fluid and, when initiating his serve, he delivers a sharp snap of the wrist at just the right moment. Because his body is relaxed, that fluid serve propels his body forward and into the court, into the game. He is all action - on offense, not defense. There is no tension in his hand and wrist. It is all working because he is focused solely on the ball. He is not so much playing where the ball is, but where it is going to be.

---

[16] Inspiringquotes.com

The price for overcoming fear is discipline. This takes time – time you might very well prefer to devote to other things. But if you want sales success, you must spend time on things that will make it happen. Like building a muscle, it takes time and concerted effort to develop higher and higher levels of fear tolerance.

> *"A competitor will find a way to win. Competitors take bad breaks and use them to drive themselves just that much harder. Quitters take bad breaks and use them as reasons to give up."*[17] *– Professional Golfer Nancy Lopez*

Playing to win is a nice way of saying you have a healthy ego and you always want to win. I plead guilty as charged. Every Saturday when I walk on that tennis court for my weekly match, I want to win; I want to beat my opponent. The best performers are those who regularly put themselves in situations requiring this kind of grit. Their courage to do this accelerates their learning through adaptation.

DIALED IN

Tennis pro Pete Sampras moved to Tampa, Florida when he was 17 years old to train. He wanted to get away from all the distractions of big cities and get himself into peak condition by playing tennis in the state with the highest humidity. "I would train myself in the middle of the day," he said, "and if I can train in that humidity in Florida, I can play anywhere in the world."[18]

Jimmy Connors, it could be argued, was not a naturally outstanding tennis player. When you scrutinize his game, he was actually very average in many ways. He was, however, consumed with a will to win. When things are not going well, when they are not playing their best, champions dig down and figure out how to win with what they have

---

[17] AZquotes.com
[18] Michael Mink & *A Champion's Mind: Lessons from a Life in Tennis* by Pete Sampras

at that moment. Champions do not get lost in worry and negative thoughts about the past, the future or the potential outcome. They let go of all that and free their mind to respond to what is happening right now. Basketball's Michael Jordan said his greatest obstacle to success was self-doubt, fear. He felt fear was strongly related to lack of concentration. When he had a critical free-throw to make, if he thought about all the people watching in the stadium and on television, he would not have been able to make the shot. He had to think of all the times in practice he executed the shot successfully, how he went through the same process, the same technique, thousands of times. He said you then forget about the outcome; you relax and perform.

> When the best tennis players are losing, they have the great ability to calmly process everything that is going wrong and reset their game by purposely slowing down. They slow their breathing; they calm mind and body. They turn off the fear switch and make small, but critical changes in their shot placement, movement on the court and, most important, they keep their focus on this point, not the next point and not the last point.

Athletes see failure as a process, not a verdict. They see it as a process that can be reversed. For them, the past is there to learn from, not to dwell on or shut out. For a salesperson, it all comes down to belief in your company and your products/services, but most importantly, belief in yourself. Without that core belief in yourself – that you are a winner – you become just another average salesperson who invariably sees only obstacles most of the time.

A salesperson may seem close to closing a sale; he has plenty of empathy and plenty of eagerness to help/serve the customer. But that's not enough. Salespeople with only empathy and no ego drive are just nice people. They also tend to be the type of people who just can't seem to close a sale. In sales, ego drive and empathy are inseparable. A lack of either one is a strong indicator of failure. What's also required is a deeply focused internal need to persuade, to overcome obstacles – to win. Average salespeople flinch at the very moment when the true winners step up, step in and continue on offense.

> In tennis, when you are in a five-setter, it's no longer about the tennis strokes. It's about who has more physical stamina and more of the sheer will to win.

All salespeople face the same rejection and the same good and bad leads. The best feed on the challenges, while the average are overwhelmed by them. And the average player will never own up to this because it is too embarrassing and too close to the truth. The "shoulda, coulda, woulda" delusional/defensive thinking does not allow for self-candor and self-honesty, so it justifies and leads to repetition of the non-closing behavior. You will have some success, but it will be a spotty record of hits and misses, in which you feel you have little to no control of the outcome.

Sales is a career in which you are confronted with your results on a daily basis. Ineffective salespeople rationalize away their failures. The strong honestly look at them, accept them and learn from them.

What the Winners Do

- Winners ignore negativity in those they interact with, and they work to eliminate it in themselves.
- Winners know they will have hot streaks where the sales are just pouring in, and they know they will have slumps where nothing seems to go right. And they know both will pass.
- Winners work through problems, whereas "whiners" work on excuses, wallow in their problems and, as a result, never get past them.
- Winners focus on jumping over obstacles, while "whiners" focus on going around obstacles.

- Winners set high standards for themselves, in terms of hard work, discipline and perseverance. They lead by example.
- Winners see setbacks as indicators to try something different or new.
- Winners are not afraid of taking that daily look in the mirror.
- Winners are results driven.
- Winners are strong self-motivators.
- Winners are almost always driven by a great purpose, and it is not money.
- Winners are not afraid of losing; losers are.
- Winners know failure is part of the process of success.
- Winners are certain; they don't equivocate.
- Winners know if you avoid failure, by default, you also avoid success.

"If you don't see yourself as a winner, then you cannot perform as a winner."[19] *– Zig Ziglar*

Having a winning attitude is all about now, all about today. It is an attitude marked by being very positive, direct and decisive. It is a belief, not a point of view. Strong salespeople know positive actions are based on positive thoughts, and so are very in tune with the mental side of the game.

Indispensable performers display an extraordinary passion to succeed and have a broad vision and understanding of the playing field. They thrive on the pace, the uncertainty and challenge of being in sales every single day. The ineffective player always has a very short-term focus, is clearly not passionate, and has more focus on the uncertainties.

Many years ago, a venue I was working in was trying to secure a large annual conference and gala. The event was valued at $400,000 (in today's dollars probably more like $1 million). I asked our general manager if he would please attend the final meeting we were having with the prospect's board and offer a few words of encouragement to help us in securing the event. The day of the meeting our general manager showed

---

[19] Brainyquote.com

up right on cue and made some very gracious remarks to all in attendance. Then he said, "You are in the best hands possible with Charlie and our teams. I personally assure you this event will be an outstanding success. I'm serious if you don't like it, then simply don't pay us."

"Wow!! Talk about being bold, direct, dialed-in, coming up with the unexpected and, of course, playing to win. Our general manager could confidently make that statement because he had total belief in our product and services, and full confidence our teams would execute. We successfully booked the event and continued to do so for the next 10 years until the organization stopped holding the event entirely.

The tangibles – listening and questioning, identifying needs and wants – most of this can be taught. However, the intangibles – empathy, overcoming fear, getting to belief and playing to win – cannot be taught. You either have it or you don't. It's all on you. All the training in the world can only succeed when the raw talent of belief, empathy and a deep desire to win are present. This is why strong salespeople can very quickly provide a clear and accurate assessment of another salesperson's ability. They immediately and intuitively sense both the strengths and the weaknesses.

All of Chapter One can be summed up in three words: **Keep It Simple.** The core selling fundamentals – the Pillars – the very framework of sales will never change. This very basic mindset will always be the benchmark of great salesmanship. The problems arise when you start to bypass, ignore and/or rewrite the fundamentals. Even worse, problems can become entrenched when you start to think particular sales situations or venues – even you – are "unique" or "different." Once you do that, it's game over for you.

So, we've said that the best salespeople listen intently to uncover real needs. They focus on building trust every step of the way, are fully engaged and present. They have an empathetic focus on customers and anticipate customer reactions and feelings throughout the sales experience. And, of course, they have that all-encompassing need to win. What else do they do to not only survive but thrive as trusted advisors by prospects and long-standing customers alike and in both good and bad markets? We will turn our attention to that in the next chapter.

Takeaways:

"People who take risks are the people you'll lose against."[20]
– John Sculley, American Businessman

*...trust is not a scarce resource, it is a fragile asset.
Once squandered it may be impossible to regain."*[21]
– August Turak

"By acting as if I was not afraid, I ceased to be afraid"[22]
Theodore Roosevelt

"Hire only rock stars not lip-syncers."[23] *–*

---

[20] Brainyquote.com
[21] "The Power of Trust," Bigthink.com, June 28, 2013.
[22] *Autobiography of Theodore Roosevelt*, Simon and Schuster (2013), p47.
[23] Jim Knight, former Director of Training, Hard Rock International, speakers.ca.

"We are what we repeatedly do. Excellence is therefore not an act but a habit."[24] — *Will Durant*

[24] *The Story of Philosophy: The Lives and Opinions of the World's Greatest Philosophers,* by Will Durant, Pocket Books – a division of Simon & Schuster, Inc. 1926.

CHAPTER 2

What Do I Have to Be All About?

"Winning is a habit. Watch your thoughts, they become your beliefs. Watch your beliefs, they become your words. Watch your words, they become your actions. Watch your actions, they become your habits. Watch your habits, they become your character. The objective is to win – fairly, squarely, decently, by the rules, but to win."[25] *– Vince Lombardi*

THE HABITS

The thing that distinguishes one performer from another is how hard he or she works. What's more, the people at the very top don't just work harder than everyone else, they work much, much harder. Think in terms of Michael Jordan. He was cut from his high school varsity basketball team. Walt Disney was fired from a newspaper job because he was told he lacked imagination. The Beatles failed to get a contract at Decca Records because the executives didn't like their sound. What made these individuals rebound from defeat? Psychologists call it "self-efficacy" – the unshakeable belief some people have that they have what it takes to succeed.

It is the same with salespeople. The best do not let anything stand in the way of succeeding and they never take any success they have for granted. They invariably think and act like they are the challengers, whether that be in solidifying or growing an existing market or

---

[25] *Investor's Business Daily*, Michael Mink – February 5,2016 and Quote Catalog

pioneering the establishment of new markets. They are out to make their mark. They are the ones who lead their teams because they are hungrier than all the rest.

As Head Coach of the New York Giants, Tom Coughlin knew this and instilled it in each of his players. In fact, he used to send the following note to each new player on day one of training:

> *"Are you interested in doing those things that are necessary to rise above mediocrity?"*[26]

Let's Define It

Habits (or routines) are defined in *Webster's Dictionary* as acquired behavioral patterns, consistently followed, learned, and repeatedly practiced until they become almost automatic. By definition, habits are about creating an environment of predictability, the structure of which allows for continuous, ongoing productivity. Anyone who is extremely good at anything practices meticulously. Athletes and indispensable salespeople show far more self-discipline than everyone else in this regard. They deliberately train themselves into good habits, carefully building the muscle memory needed to perform at the highest level, the first time and every time. Routine…Habit…the words are interchangeable. The important thing is to do it. This chapter goes right at it. If you want to change, first change your actions and your thinking and belief will follow. Let's take a look at each.

1. The Knowledge Habit

Knowledge is power, and the basis of that power is curiosity. A salesperson who is genuinely curious about his or her clients and prospective clients will sell more, pure and simple. Reading, research and indulging in new experiences all rely on a curious mind and fuel one's knowledge base. People who tend to have a fixed mindset are usually not curious.

---

[26] *USA Today*, August 22, 2013.

Essentially, they have stopped seeking knowledge. By contrast, those who have a growth outlook pretty much believe they can do anything. One of the basics of the knowledge habit is to:

Constantly dig for information on companies, organizations and individuals. Which companies are moving into your area and which are moving out? How many events does a company do in your area or across the country? Who is on their board? Does anyone in your company have a relationship with or access to board members of these companies? As you gain more and more knowledge in this area, you will start to see the overlap between key corporate figures and the boards of various fundraising organizations. You will home in on the new companies and sectors where you want to focus your solicitation efforts. This kind of knowledge focuses you. It helps you lock in. It gives you a base to work from, even before you have spoken with or met the potential customer. It gives you a basis for building rapport in the very critical early stages of the first encounter.

In tennis, you need good leg (calf) strength to launch yourself into action, place you on offense, and allow yourself to properly return your next shot with pace and proper placement. To develop this leg strength requires regular squats and leg lifts. The same concept applies to gaining knowledge. It is said, for example, that Warren Buffet reads three annual reports a day – over 500 pages – to hone his business knowledge. And, like compound interest, knowledge builds up daily.

When you have developed this kind of knowledge, it shows. It also gives you that little bit of leverage which, in turn, gives you more control and a broader vision of the playing field. This is when you are truly able to start dictating play.

Know Your Competition. You must know your competition cold. There have been only a few occasions where I did not already know before asking where a potential customer had previously hosted their events, the competition's general offerings, pros and cons, and how my venue stacked up to theirs. On those few occasions though, I had to think immediately about all the pros and cons of the particular venue, while still carrying on what appeared to be a low-key conversation with the potential customer. You have more power and authority if you know this information, even if it is never mentioned in the discussion. In addition, you need to know everything about all other potential competitors for your business.

Case in point: For many years I worked with an out of town fundraising organization on their annual gala, until one year they informed me they had decided to move their event to another venue. I stayed calm and listened carefully as they told me all their reasons for wanting to make the change. I then responded by saying I could certainly understand and accept some of their reasoning for this decision. However, I also needed to point out that no matter what the contact at the other venue had told them, the other venue simply could not accommodate the size of their event, based on its published square footage. They couldn't argue with my calm demeanor and immediate logical explanation of the numbers. As a result, we retained the business.

Why is it so important to have this information right then and there? Well, during your initial meeting or phone call, you are, for the most part, receiving unedited, unfiltered information from the prospect. Your questions might surprise them, and their answers will tend to be more unrehearsed. You can also ask follow-up questions, based on the competitive weaknesses you discover, and see what their responses are to these, as well.

There's a reason why the "SWOT" analysis has been around for so many years. It's an excellent tool for knowing your competition. Unfortunately, some salespeople do not take advantage of its immense value. How does it work? Simply create a spreadsheet for each of your major competitors, outlining in detail their **S**trengths, **W**eaknesses, **O**pportunities (for you) and **T**hreats (to you). The very best salespeople keep these spreadsheets handy, and update and review them regularly until they have almost memorized the major points. Tennis star Serena Williams does a thorough review and evaluation of her opponent with her coach before each match – who she is, how she plays, her current strengths, weaknesses and patterns of play. Then she works with her coach on tactics to counter each. As a result, Serena is poised to win before she even meets her opponent on the court.

Almost Out of the Game. I will always remember an organization I had worked with for 10 years – we hosted their annual fundraising dinner for 900 guests. It was a great piece of business and benefited a great cause. In late June, I called to remind the client our confirmation letter needed to be signed for next year's dinner. I was totally caught off guard to hear him say, "Well Charlie, I'm sorry but we're not going back to your facility next year. We've had 10 great dinners with you, and we have certainly enjoyed working with you. But we have brought on a new executive director and some new board members who want to go in a different direction. We really need to change it up."

I didn't know what to say. I was stunned. I knew I was losing the business, but I really did not know much else at that point. I did, however, have the good sense to ask, "Where are you going to host the event?" He told me it would be with one of our major competitors a few blocks away. Well, when I got off the phone, I vividly recall sitting there in absolute shock. I thought, "How dare they do this to me after all these years when I have always been so good to them!" The next (and saner) thing I did was to walk up the street to the other venue. I knew the venue well, but I wanted to walk through the facility again and try to see it through the eyes of my now-lost client. When I got there, I noticed some workers were erecting scaffolding around one corner of the building and I asked what was going on. It turns out the venue was starting a major renovation and the scaffolding would be covering the entire building for at least a year and a half. I immediately called my client (I didn't email or leave a message) and asked if they were aware of this situation. Long pause…no, they were not. The hotel in question had violated an implied trust that the building would be in the same condition and appearance in May 2009 as it was in June 2008. That bit of knowledge was my opening. My competitor proceeded to lose the business and we retained the account. Strong salespeople leave nothing to chance and never take the first no as the final no.

Know Your Own Operation. Know your products. Know your catering menus, a few domestic and imported wines, and some general catering trends. You don't have to be an expert, that's why you have an Executive

Chef. But you do have to have some basic understanding of what is going on in your operations and your industry, as well as what works for a variety of events of differing size, ages and make up. You need to know from an operational standpoint what the best menu options are for a dinner of 1,400 vs. 300. And you must be able to hold the banquet operational people accountable for certain standards of service. Similarly, you need to know your own facility. You would be surprised how many salespeople don't. In each of the five major facilities I have worked in my career, I spent over three weeks just learning the physical space – how it was laid out, how it worked, what kinds of events worked best in the space and why. I made sure I was comfortable with the hotel itself before I tried to sell it. More to the point, I sold myself on the facility before trying to sell it to someone else. The same applies to the catering event scheduling screen – commonly referred to as "the diary." Do you know how to effectively read the diary – all the little ins and outs needed to work in a piece of business, particularly when it appears there is no meeting space available?

A salesman came to me once asking: How do you get a car into the hotel and up to the Grand Ballroom? It was a good question, and I was certainly willing to answer it for him. What I didn't realize initially was that while I was talking with the salesman, the client was waiting for him in the reception area. In other words, the salesman had to step away from his appointment to find out the answer. By the way, did I mention, the appointment was with a major car company? Although the salesperson was eventually able to provide the correct information, the question remains: How confident and sure of himself was he when doing so? And what was the non-verbal communication to the potential customer? Certainly, there was a good chance the customer's first impression was not a favorable one.

In some instances, operational managers will have a concern that a salesperson may not have as much of an in-depth knowledge as they should about some of the operational issues of a specific event. And, in many cases, their analysis is correct. These individuals do not spend the time required to thoroughly learn the key aspects of their facilities. They know a few of the most basic points and think that will see them through. As a result, you see salespeople who are tentative with their operational staff and worse, even more tentative with their customers. You will often hear, "Let me check with our culinary team," or "Let me ask my banquet captain or my event manager." If you do not know then how can you expect these departments to execute to any standard? How can you expect your customer or potential customer to have confidence that you will deliver?

People start to interpret all the tentativeness as stalling, and that you just do not know much. The perception they have of you is you are – albeit – a nice person, but you are hesitant, tentative and not knowledgeable. You cannot, therefore, be entrusted with handling their business.

Know the Score. Know where you are on your booking pace; know where you are in comparison to your actual sales from last year vs. your actual sales for this year. Know if you're up, know if you're down. And if you're down, know how much new business you need this year to counteract any lost business from last year. What is your year-over-year average of new versus repeat bookings and is that ratio in line year to date? If not, what can you reach for to bring that ratio in line? Such "numbers knowledge" builds your confidence, focuses your efforts and helps eliminate fear.

When developing yearly game plans, the very first thing I always asked each team member to do was to make two lists: 1. A list of accounts (with revenue) they lost for the coming year, and 2. A list of new accounts (with revenue) they'd booked for the coming year.

If the difference was a minus (it rarely is a plus), then that team member had to address how he would: A. Recoup the lost revenue, and B. Outline specific target accounts (with revenue) to achieve that.

Given this very fundamental game plan guideline, imagine receiving the following email thread from a salesperson in late August:

August 27

I am very concerned about this quarter. I may be $200-225K below. I will check to see what was turned definite

*in last year's third quarter and compare why it is so down
this year.*

September 10

*I analyzed what was turned definite last year for 3rd quarter
and saw there were several groups not returning.*

Total: $327,650 lost business for third quarter.

September 10

*Any leads for the remainder of the year you do not need,
please send them my way.*

Let's review this correspondence: First of all, he was "concerned"? What about "startled? He would not have been as "concerned" if he had done his analysis sooner. And, "...leads I do not need"? Does this sound like a salesperson? Do I have $300k in "extra" leads? Even if I did, is he really going to close the business by the end of the quarter – in two weeks? Notice, too, it took two weeks from the initial email to do the "analysis" of what was lost from last year.

Solid sales performers *always* know where they are on their booking goals and actual sales year over year. They naturally and intuitively analyze where they are on the playing field at critical points throughout the year. They regularly see how their sales are shaping up by quarter and year to date for both their current year sales and their future bookings for the next year. They ask themselves, "Where am I short? What can I do for short-term success in this quarter? And if not this quarter, what can I secure for the next quarter to counterbalance the shortfall? If next year is the problem, what hasn't played out successfully and what back-up plan do I have to recoup?" These performers don't start executing their game plan in Q1 of the new year; they have already started in Q4 (or even sooner) of last year. They do an ongoing and detailed review of goals, dollars etc., throughout the year, while also focusing on the bigger picture with forward-thinking analysis and vision. They do not neglect one at the expense of the other. Great salespeople have this kind of conversation with themselves all the time.

Know a Specific Market. What about the banking industry? What about the insurance, financial or legal industries? What about the LGBTQ, Hispanic, Sports or African-American communities and markets? What about weddings and proms? Kosher and ethnic markets? For each of these and more, you must ask yourself:

- Am I the expert?
- Am I the go-to person in my company for this particular market?
- Do I know the key players in different organizations within the market and, more to the point, can I reach them?
- Do I know the key players that can impact an entire market?
- Do I own the market, or was it just assigned to me way back when?

Can you say with confidence you are a specialist in a particular market? If you have that kind of in-depth knowledge, it not only gives you tremendous self-confidence but a significant competitive edge. This is an advantage that translates into more lead generation and ultimately more sales. Customers really like it if you say you are a "specialist." It makes them feel good about themselves; they feel they are getting more value for their money. And, of course, it also contributes to your being known within your organization (even your industry) as an indispensable performer. Of course, you must back it up and demonstrate your expertise.

Is the sports market realistically a good market for you? Is that your niche? Although being a fan is a good start, playing or coaching a sport is even better. Be it tennis, hockey, golf or soccer, if you play or coach a sport on a regular basis or are an avid fan, when you meet a customer who has a similar intense interest, you will almost immediately establish a much stronger comfort level and rapport. Your relationship with that customer is now on a totally different level. In sales, this translates into trust, and trust leads to sales.

How about Asian-American organizations? That's my niche. Now what would an American guy of Irish descent from Queens know about Asian-American organizations? Well it turns out, quite a bit. The Asian-American population is growing in huge numbers in New York City. I do a tremendous amount of reading about China, Japan, Taiwan and Korea. I follow the political and economic trends in those countries, and the impact it has on immigrants in the United States. I read all the local newspapers that advertise Asian events, and I attend many Asian events in New York and in the outer boroughs of Brooklyn, Queens and Long Island. My wife was born and raised in Taiwan, and two of our four children are of direct Taiwanese descent. We live in a mixed community of American and Asian-American neighbors. If you were to visit our home, you would be exposed to many Asian customs and traditions, as well as to some of the very best Taiwanese home-cooking you will have ever eaten. I therefore have an ongoing and direct experience with the transition Asian-American people go through when they immigrate to the United States.

When my wife and I attend Asian-American fundraising or social events, we feel an immediate connection. My direct knowledge, understanding and practice of these cultural traditions helps me to further build my own relationship with each person I meet. For example, ballroom dancing, golf and ping-pong are very big within the Asian-American community. So, at these gatherings, I make it a point to say that I play golf and ping-pong, and/or that my wife and I enjoy ballroom dancing. Having something in common beats "like" every time.

To sum it up on "Knowledge," too many salespeople don't, in a substantive way, really know their products and services, their competitors, their markets or their numbers. Too often they say, "I think so," or 'Let me check on that," or worse: "Let me talk with my director about that." You are the one who needs to know where and how to access the knowledge and how to implement it. You must keep growing your knowledge bank throughout your entire career if you expect to be a highly successful salesperson. A confident salesperson is always prepared. If you are prepared, you will thrive. If not, you will only survive – if that. And, unfortunately, in sales, too many are doing the latter.

2. The Connecting Habit

This is a biggie: Actually talking to a live human being. It seems comical that we even have to discuss this, but thanks to texting, email and voicemail, speaking directly to a person has become increasingly rare, even in sales. Facetime is critical. Face-to-face conversations or, at a minimum, telephone conversations with customers and/or potential customers, are a "must" in sales. This familiarity contributes to building rapport, trust and sales.

I recall a salesperson who was trying to book a holiday party for a major financial company for about 1,200 guests. It was worth over $300,000. The sales manager never sat down though to have any real discussion of the prospective customer's needs; he only conducted a very brief (less than 30-minute) site inspection with the event coordinator. The excuse, I was told: "The prospect was on a tight time schedule, planning to look at four venues in three hours that day." Following the site inspection and, within hours, the salesperson followed up with a written proposal. This is when the "thinking, wishing, hoping something happens game" commenced. The salesperson waited and hoped to hear back from whom they thought was the customer. The salesperson sent a follow-up email a week later. The contact emailed back saying they were still reviewing everything. Turns out, the event coordinator was not the decision-maker and not – it seemed – even a key influencer, even though the contact gave the salesperson the impression he was.

Finally, one day the contact sent an email at 1:14 p.m., thanking the salesperson for his interest, but informing him they had decided to go in "a totally different direction." They would, however, definitely keep us in mind for future events. At 1:15 p.m., the salesperson sent back an email thanking the contact for letting him know, and asking ever-so-gently where they decided to do the event. Not surprisingly, the contact never responded to that email. $300,000 went down the drain, following not one phone call nor even an attempted follow-up conversation with the decision-maker. Bottom line: The salesperson allowed himself to be treated like a commodity, conducted himself like he was selling a commodity, and the result speaks for itself. When you find yourself in situations where someone does not want to connect, the logical question must always be, "If not, then why not?"

> *News Flash:* Email communication breeds email responses (if that). How about just picking up the phone?

Emails and very brief meetings and site inspections are convenient and enable basic transactions, but they fall short, in terms of establishing relationships of trust. These transactions are one dimensional; they offer only very surface level communication and more than play into the illusion of selling. There is a level of integrity and empathy required to build real business relationships, and face-to-face interaction is the only way you can do it. You only win points (and sales) with human interactions. Or as Warren Buffet says:

"You will never see eye to eye if you never meet face to face."[27]

Move those Feet...Getting Out on the Dance Floor

Attending business and charitable events is a great way to connect; it helps you further establish your presence in the community and your industry. Attending with your spouse adds an even more personal dimension versus bringing a work colleague. This is not always possible, but when the option presents itself it's good to take advantage of it. After seeing you at one event after another, key people start to sense you are a "player" in your company; that you are in that smaller select group of people who can actually make things happen.

I once attended a major dinner event for a Korean American

---

[27] Meetings Mean Business, June 8, 2015.

organization at one of our competitors' venues. I connected with two gentlemen, exchanged business cards and had a brief conversation. The end-result of that chance encounter: They booked a dinner with me for another Korean organization for 1,000 people for $165,000 – all based on a coincidental meeting at an event.This booking further lead to two other major Korean-American organizations moving their events to our venue as well.

Unfortunately, some salespeople are reluctant – even afraid – to make such direct contact. They'll say, "I just don't have time to do this kind of solicitation/networking stuff." If they do attend such an event, they go with one or two other colleagues, all of whom sit together. They don't really reach out to anyone, and they don't scour the seating list or journal to see if any other potential clients or prospects are attending. They usually come in the next day offering a lot of generalities about the event and always bring up whatever negatives they noticed with the food, service or the facility. All well and good, but the most important opportunity – client and potential client contact – is lost. It's all cover lines to cover their fear: Fear of making the first move, fear of making a mistake, fear of embarrassing themselves. These are all legitimate feelings, all understandable, and all of which must be eliminated. Your sales depend on it.

3. The (Probing) Questioning Habit

As discussed, knowledge and connecting initiate sales success. With probing questions, though, you can take the conversation to a whole new level. In combination with all we have covered so far, powerful, assertive, challenging questions position you as an influencer, a person who can make things happen. When you do this, you start to shape the conversation while building rapport and trust. Without offending or alienating a prospective customer, you can very effectively ask some of the following questions:

Game-Changer Questions

- What has held you back from going with us before?
- What will it take for you to give us serious consideration?
- What will make it a success for you?
- Did I make any progress today in helping you see our venue as a strong option for your future events? If the answer is no, the follow-up question would be: Where did I miss the boat on this?
- What do you think we should do next?
- Do you feel confident with what I have presented to you?
- What does a company have to do to secure your business (or earn your loyalty)?
- What should I make sure does not happen at your wedding?

Note: Back to tennis, these and similar questions help you establish your presence on the "court" and most effectively "dictate play." The questions are direct, transparent and require answers.

How about when meeting with or talking with a bride on the telephone. Ask her: "So, how did he go about asking you?" Most salespeople don't ask that, at least not early on. Most are still reciting the standard: What date would you be interested in? How many people? Afternoon or evening? The fact is, most brides are usually pleasantly surprised by the question and eager to tell you.

Sales trainers often advise you to "be aggressive and come right out and ask for the business." In truth, literally asking for the business causes more problems than it solves. I cringe whenever I hear this advice. Inexperienced directors of marketing tend to be the ones who advise this and say it often. In my experience, when someone asks this question, it is way too early in the sales process and it puts both the customer and the salesperson in an embarrassing and awkward position. Think of a dating website, for example. After you scan a few profiles you might land on one that draws your attention and think perhaps this one is worth exploring. So you send off a little email, you reach out to her, you might even exchange one or two more emails and then suggest speaking by phone or meeting for a cup of coffee. At this point, however, you would certainly not ask her to marry you, even though that may be your ultimate goal.

Here is an example of an uncomfortable, yet probing, question I have asked potential customers many times (after doing all the necessary legwork): "I think I have done a pretty good job of finding out what your needs are for this event. I have also presented you with a very detailed thorough plan to address those needs. At this point, do you feel comfortable with what I have presented? Do you feel confident enough to select us?" Now that is a powerful question and it certainly conveys a clear expectation of an honest answer. What's even more powerful is to shut up after you ask it and wait for the response, even if there is an uncomfortable silence. If the answer is "Not yet," you at least have an opportunity to fix it. But you must wait for the answer, and you must listen to the answer.

Note: Think of game changer questions as your attempt to keep things ridiculously simple. They cut through the clutter and all the polite bureaucratic conversation to get to the truth.

The Great Nemesis of Sales: Questioning Yourself

A few years ago, at the Masters Golf Tournament, a great player – Doug Spieth – was leading the pack with a 5-stroke lead when he "choked," quadruple bogeying the 12th hole (a par 3). Victory was his, but self-inflicted pressure and stress broke down his entire game and he ended up losing. At the US Tennis Open in 2012, Victoria Azarenka was serving for the match (one point away from victory!) when she lost her focus and her entire game broke down. On the other hand, her opponent Serena Williams dug down deep, refused to accept defeat, came back strong and won not only the point but went on to win the entire match.

In both examples, great competitors let their focus waiver. They started to second guess themselves. They were no longer playing to win; they were no longer in the now. They let the fear of losing get the best of them. They overthought their shots. They were, in fact, no longer taking the necessary risks required to win; they were just trying to protect their leads. It's the same in sales. When you are not asking assertive and probing questions, you are hiding – hiding from the truth and "choking." Asking the right questions will get you where you need to go. Be direct, proactive and straightforward. All those times you say, "What if…?" or "Supposing they…" or "I'm not sure, I'd better…." you are, by default, moving backwards.

When you are moving forward, you show an expectation of an honest response by your very presence and demeanor. People appreciate that, and you will get an honest answer almost 100% of the time.

4. The Managing Time Habit

Most people get sucked into the illusion they can multitask. Some even wear it as a badge of honor. The reality? It is the single best way to undermine productivity and your quality of life. The brain is hard wired to do a single task at a time. Edward Hallowell, author of *Driven to Distraction at Work* says there is an epidemic of attention deficit at work, encouraged by our culture. "The symptoms," he says, "are a persistent feeling of being rushed, an inability to give full attention to our thoughts, a tendency toward impatience or boredom and a habit of hopping from task to task. People valiantly try to keep track of more and more data than even the most accomplished human brain could possibly accommodate."[28] Sound familiar? Sounds to me like a person who is not in charge of his day, but whose day is in charge of him.

Too many salespeople allow themselves to buy into the concept that being very busy means they are highly productive and very important. Indispensable salespeople, however, learned a long time ago that being very busy is a loser's game. On the contrary, being highly productive is what matters and really counts in the end.

The simple answer to all of this is we need to figure out what is worth paying attention to and when. This simple thing, though, turns

---

[28] Inspiring Quotes.com

out to be incredibly hard to do. We tend to sabotage ourselves without even knowing it. Why? Because we don't like to tell anyone "No." Being available and responsive is considered a good thing in our culture, and responding right away to a phone call or an email makes us feel good, productive and accomplished. These things deceive us, though. The deception is because these things are urgent, they are important. When you step back from it for a few moments, however, you can clearly see the work is "working you." The trick is to balance being responsive with the need to complete critically important projects. In other words, "The art of being wise, "as philosopher William James wrote over 100 years ago, "is the art of knowing what to overlook." [29]

WHERE IS YOUR FOCUS?

The best salespeople establish their priorities early in the day, if not the night before. Then they judge all interruptions against those priorities. This planning ahead does not use up time, it creates it.

How? Focus on your objectives, not on activities. Your most important activities are those that help you accomplish your objectives. Failure to focus on objectives will lead to activity traps. Oh, you'll be very busy, but you won't accomplish much. There are only a few vital things; most things are trivial. It's the vital things, though, that produce contribution and value.

Often, you'll hear someone say he or she is "not a morning person," or they have the most energy late in the day. Say what you will, but the scientific data does not back this up.[30] Charlie Munger – a financial partner of Warren Buffet – decided very early in his career to do something for his most important client: himself. Every day from 6 a.m. to 7 a.m. he would do nothing else but focus on and think about matters that

---

[29] *The Principles of Psychology*, William James, p22.
[30] Nolan G. Pope's *Review of Economics and Statistics* outlined a lengthy report with statistical data to support his contention that productivity is higher in the morning than the afternoon, © March 2016 The President and Fellows of Harvard College and MIT, p1-11.

pertained to him only.[31] Alex Soo Jung-Kim Pang – author of *Rest: Why You Get More Done When You Work Less* says very productive people do their most critical work early in the morning when they are free of distractions, have time to think, and are the most alert.[32]

EARLY BIRDS

I had a customer who organized a very large dinner for people in the Wall Street financial industry. When I first approached him about considering our venue for his event he said, "Yes, I'd like to meet with you, preferably before I go to work. But I get in at 6:00 a.m. before the market opens. I'm not sure you get in that early. "I immediately said, "That's fine," and we agreed to meet at 6:15 a.m. I usually don't get in quite that early in the morning, but I knew what I was doing. I was working on his time schedule and I was getting one step up on my competitors, who usually come in around 8:45 a.m. or 9:30 a.m. I was keyed into his needs from the get-go. I was also showing I shared a similar work ethic. As a result, from that very first meeting, I sensed that he and I were connecting. I ended up booking that piece of business and rebooked it for 12 more years (a total of about $9.5 million dollars). That's pretty good for simply getting in a little bit early. Incidentally, every single meeting I had with that organization thereafter was at 6:15 a.m. Lesson learned:

> If you're going to go after the "Big Kahuna," you have to create the time, and you have to play by *his* rules.

---

[31] Published by Basic Books, an imprint of Perseus Books, a division of PBG Publishing, LLC, a subsidiary of Hachette Book Group, Inc.
[32] Published by The Presidents and Fellows of Harvard College & MIT, p 1-11, March 2016.

My Early A.M. Drill

When you focus on time management, you are focused on results. Strong salespeople know this. They are all about being organized and punctual. What an observer sees as persistence is – to a degree – a reflection of that salesperson's time management and organizational skills. For example, by 8:30 a.m. – Monday through Friday – I had accomplished the following:

- I had had a full, healthy breakfast.
- I had taken some time for quiet reflection and prayer.
- I had done some basic exercise for about 25 minutes.
- I had showered, shaved and dressed professionally to meet the day ahead.
- On my morning commute, I had read part of a good book that had absolutely nothing to do with business.
- Once in the office, I either reviewed a contract before I sent it out or I put together a contract to be sent out that morning.
- I had placed two calls to customers, whom I knew would be in early too, and whom I knew were open to receiving calls at that hour. Or, I would answer a few routine calls from the prior day that only required I leave a voicemail message with basic information.
- If I had a group meeting in the hotel, I would go up and greet the client very early and make sure he was comfortable before things got hectic for him. I also would check the set-up and talk to the operating departments to make sure all was going according to plan.
- I would then pick-up the four major newspapers I read every day and skim through one of them for business leads and/or articles of interest. I would skim the other papers periodically throughout the rest of the day.

The Reality: It is your (and only your) responsibility to allocate the 168 hours a week (1,440 minutes per day) each of us has available. The only thing you can control is your time. Time goes where you tell it to go. Ultimately, it is your game plan, and you are the one – *the only one* – who can execute it. True sales professionals eliminate distractions, have a very positive energy that touches all they do, and start to work right away when they arrive to work because they have a plan.

> *"The difference between successful people and very successful people is the very successful people say no to almost everything"*[33] *– Warren Buffet*

Please see Appendix A for additional time management tips.

#5. DOING THE LITTLE THINGS HABIT

When you pay attention to the little things, people sense you are different, that you are authentic, that you are truly listening and that you are sensitive to those around you. They see you as someone who can make things happen. You stand out from all the rest. *This is the zone that you want to live in!* Find those moments, those little touches. The focus is on them, not on you. But remember, it must be subtle, sincere and real.

A few examples:

- Answer your own telephone as often as possible.
- Return calls quickly – even on your days off. It promotes respect from customers. Record daily voicemail greetings, including the date. It shows you are on the ball.
- "Can I help you?" is pretty standard. How about "How can I help you today?" Isn't that more positive, more direct, more open, more in-the-moment? Doesn't that sentence better convey your sincere desire to be of service today, right now?
- When asked for something by a customer, before establishing a date or method of delivery, make sure to ask, "What is most convenient for you?" Most people will be pleasantly surprised.

---

[33] Goodreads.com

- If you are returning a customer call from the day before, always apologize for not being able to call them back yesterday.
- When sending a contract, refer to it as a confirmation letter. The word "contract" can make people feel tense.
- Say thank you often. You will be amazed at how many times this most obvious little thing is taken for granted or, worse, the salesperson assumes the other person knows you are thankful. Find ways to sincerely thank the customer right away.
- When a customer signs a major contract, why not visit the customer with your general manager, just to say a heartfelt and sincere "thank you for having the confidence in us to select our venue," and to emphasize that we will not let you down. That's it. It's simple and it has real impact.
- Make a point of writing notes to yourself as you notice small details. It heightens your awareness and ability to implement those details.
- Send anniversary cards to customers, especially on first and second wedding anniversaries. The same with birthday cards for key customers.
- Respect other people's time.
- If you have to say you don't know the answer on something say, "I'm not sure, but I will find out."
- Send a thank you note when a major prospective customer has come in for a meeting with you and a site inspection.
- Send a welcome letter to key VIPs on any large group you book.

Challenge yourself to come up with a few more. It's amazing what you will come up with once you truly focus on the little things.

LITTLE THINGS TO NOT SAY OR DO

- **Don't say to customers, "No problem," "Yeah" "Absolutely" or "Sure."** These words are overly friendly and too casual, and are used, in general, way too often. Substitute professional-sounding words, such as, "My pleasure" and "Of course." If you start thinking of yourself as a 5-star and not a 2-star individual, you will clearly see the disconnect with the former.

- **Don't say "Correct."** I don't know about you, but when a salesperson repeatedly says "Correct" to a customer, it feels a little bit like the salesperson is telling the customer that he or she did, indeed, give the correct answer. It also sounds a bit robotic. The net result is it doesn't help, and it could conceivably hurt your odds of developing rapport, so why risk it?

- **Never say "Let me talk to my boss,"** especially when discussing price. You immediately lose credibility and cause the customer to wonder, "Why am I talking to you? I should be talking to your boss."

- **Never give a direct "No" to a customer.** Soften it. Say, "We could do…" (this or that) and highlight the pros and cons of each option as you try to persuade the person to agree with you. Starting your response with "Usually," also serves to soften your response.

- **Never say "What does your company do?"** You are supposed to know.

- **Never say, "I would definitely like to try to get that done for you today."** You think I'm kidding? I've heard it, and more than once!

- **When scheduling appointments with customers, don't say I have a group in that day, so I will be pretty busy.** It's not about you. You always want each customer to feel they are your focus.

- **Don't refer to customers as "You guys,"** especially if the customers are older than you. They may be spending anywhere from $100k to over $1 million dollars with you and deserve to be referenced more professionally. One possible exception: If both you and your client are 25 to 35 years old, it works. Otherwise, don't do it.

- **Don't say, "It is all complete, it's just on the director's desk for final approval."** I came across this in an email correspondence from a sales manager to a customer. Wow, talk about abdicating your power and implying their business is not that important. It has the sense of, "We will let you know when we get to it."

6. The Regenerating Habit

Top performers balance actions that require total concentration with activities (exercise, sleep, reflection) that allow for complete relaxation. This pattern boosts creativity and helps ideas and solutions come to the surface. It helps you recharge, refresh, bounce back, rejuvenate or – what I consider the best description – breathe new life into whatever you are doing. Although often overlooked, health, exercise, time with family and friends and proper sleep all have tremendous benefits. Revitalizing your mind, body and spirit – the personal side – feeds into the professional side and vice-versa. Indispensable performers see food as fuel for their "engine" and sleep for recovery and adding balance. They also know they cannot be effective decision-makers unless they connect with people and pursuits outside of work. Smiles, laughter and conversation are all natural antidepressants, which family and friends can provide.

Energy is also paramount for any indispensable performer. Energy is where performance comes from. You can significantly increase your energy through exercise – another potent antidepressant. It lowers blood pressure, releases tension/anxiety, sharpens the mind, increases your stamina, lowers stress and helps you be "in the now." The more you consciously live this way, the happier and more successful you will be.

Aim for consistent – not necessarily, intensive – exercise. Find "your" time of day to exercise: Early morning, at noon or right after work. Stretch, do yoga, take a 30-minute walk, bike ride or swim. Whatever it is, make sure it is realistic and something you can see yourself doing consistently day after day, six to nine months from now. Conversely, lack of exercise contributes to lack of focus, lethargy, depression and poor health overall.

Playing a sport creates even more energy and balance. It helps you tremendously in terms of focus and staying in the moment. Through sports, you learn so much about overcoming obstacles, anticipating, coming from behind and being even more in the "now. The important concept of "Don't think, play" is learned in sports. When you do this, you create pace and momentum, and learn to adjust on the fly. This, in turn, diminishes anxiety and fear, elevates mood, enhances problem-solving and boosts productivity.

Daily Reflection

Hand in hand with exercise and proper sleep is spiritual recharging. This can take many forms – daily prayer, meditation, spiritual reading or quiet reflection. Whichever form you choose, daily reflection provides a sense of perspective and adds a certain calmness to your mind and spirit. Some refer to it as "mindfulness." Others simply call it taking time not to talk, still others refer to it as being in the presence of the God of their understanding. The idea is to sit for about 10 to 15 minutes daily, focus simply on your breathing and just "be." If other thoughts enter your mind during this time, just keep coming back to a focus on your breathing. Most people will tell you that this process helps increase their focus overall and makes them sharper and more effective. At the same time, it helps them experience a decrease in stress and an equally significant increase in work-life balance.

Returning emails and constantly checking all your devices, shopping or watching television does not make you happy; reflection and being around family and friends does. Even just turning off your cell phone for one day a week (for example, on the Sabbath) is very rejuvenating; it redirects your attention and focus to the people around you.

In addition, reflect on all the wonderful people who have been placed in your life. Aren't children a gift? Don't they help you stay much more grounded in today, more humble and much less self-centered? If not daily, at least once a week mentally review all that you are grateful for. You start to realize all those so-called problems you have are just not that big nor important. In many cases, they're not even problems at all.

SELF-CRITIQUE

Part of regenerating is doing a regular assessment of your own behavior. Some call this a "self-critique," a kind way of saying you need to be absolutely honest with yourself. If nothing else, a self-critique helps in your mental recovery and helps you become more resilient. Any good salesperson critiques himself and asks others for their honest input on a regular basis. Self-critique can be employed on three levels:

Level 1: Be Candid

Ask Yourself:

* Does this person buy, need or want <u>exactly</u> what I am selling?
* Is this person showing some <u>real</u> interest in possibly buying from <u>me?</u>
* Can this person afford to host the event with us? Does he/she have the money?

The best salespeople welcome these questions; they always want to avoid that dangerous trap of self-delusion they see so many others fall into.

Level 2: Analyze

Ask Yourself:

- How did that call really go?
- Why didn't he return my call?
- Maybe if I left a more engaging message, he would have called me back.
- Is he really interested or am I just lying to myself?
- Why did I lose that event to X?
  - Was it because I was outsold?
  - Was it because they didn't have enough confidence, trust and belief in me that I would deliver?

It can be tempting to want to believe that you lost a piece of business because the competition lowered their price, and the average performer often succumbs to this way of thinking. He prefers to say this than to be honest and admit he was outsold, or the competition created a better value package. You owe it to yourself to ask yourself these questions and to, on a broader basis, think through what is going on in your industry today and what could be going on in the future. You want to honestly evaluate these items in the frankest terms. If you don't, you run the risk of playing the game in the "think, wish, hope something happens" zone, and there are quite a few examples of this around. Worse yet, if you do not question yourself in this regard, you will not grow. You will end up being one of that vast number of people who are always watching what happens or wondering what happened, but who never actually make things happen.

Level 3: Just Think

You might be tempted to call this a luxury. Well then, schedule some luxury time for yourself. Set aside some of that valuable time in your busy day for you and you alone. Just think with a blank mind and don't censor anything. A study by the University of California Santa Barbara found people who engaged in daydreaming and abstract thought were 41% better at creative thinking. People who reported positive daydreaming were also the least depressed, and they also had a proclivity to achieve long-term goals. In one study, 72% of people indicated they got their best ideas in the shower – perhaps not coincidentally, the one place you cannot use a smartphone. The best part of this "Just Think" exercise is it opens your mind and takes you out of the "What if" zone. Instead – and in combination with exercise, proper sleep, and proper reflection – you increasingly start to play the game in the "now," in the "So what?" zone. It frees your mind to focus only on the "ball," which goes right back to the "Don't Think, Play" mindset.

All of Chapter 2 can be summed up in four words: "Take the

Ball Early." In tennis, if you do not step in early, with your racquet out in front of your body, it is impossible to hit a shot down the line. Competitive tennis players instinctively come up to the net more often and more quickly than do their counterparts. In sports, when you hesitate, you come up short and lose. It's the same in sales.

If you practice and develop the habits outlined in this chapter, you will be taking an important and aggressive step forward. In concert, these habits will place you in the game, not late to the game. Think of Blackberry: at one point their share of the cellphone market was larger than that of Samsung and Apple combined. Today, it's less than 5%. They were late to the new game.

A lot of people continue to do what they do because they are most comfortable with what they already know. Athletes and good salespeople know differently and live differently. General Douglas MacArthur summed it up best over 70 years ago:

"The history of failure in war can almost be summed up in two words: Too Late. Too late in comprehending the deadly purpose of a potential enemy; too late in realizing the mortal danger; too late in preparedness; too late in uniting all possible forces for resistance; too late in standing with one's friends."[34]

As applied to sales, without consistent application of the essential habits, you will be:

- Too late anticipating both danger and opportunity.
- Too late in seeing both of them in the first place.
- Too late in preparing for either one.
- Too late in being able to take action.

Don't let this be you. Play to win.

---

[34] Adapted from *No Substitute for Victory* by Theodore Kinni and Donna Kinni. Published by Pearson Education, Inc., publishing as Financial Times Prentice Hall, 2005.

"If you want success over a long period of time you don't start a business or initiative with the idea of how do I maximize profits. You start with how can I create the most value for others?"[35] *— Charles Koch, Koch Industries*

[35] *Investor's Business Daily*, Julie Vallone February 25, 2012

CHAPTER 3

What Are Buyers All About?

Now, let's turn our attention to the buyers. First of all, who are they? Is everybody a potential customer? Not necessarily. A lot is riding on your identifying and understanding who your current customers are and – even more important – who, realistically, could become your new customers. There are only five types of buyers you will interact with on a consistent basis. They are:

1. **Rock Stars.** This is your base. These are all those wonderful customers who provide you with solid annual repeat business: Annual association dinners, holiday parties, business conferences and fundraising events. These are truly your best clients. They are extremely happy with your services, trust you implicitly, count on you to deliver, and are very loyal. Their mantra is "If it ain't broke, don't fix it." They also take every opportunity to refer potential new customers your way. We all need these Rock Stars, and the more the merrier.

2. **Lookers.** This is generally a pretty happy group, but they are willing to explore. They are open to the possibility of a better deal or a better way. If you are very observant, you can detect an ever-so-slight hesitation and, perhaps, even an uneasiness in their voices about their current event venue. They seem to be questioning the value of what they are currently doing and getting.

3. **Shoppers.** They are not a happy group. They are dissatisfied. They are upset with their present situation and are actively looking for/exploring other options for their events.

4. **Dealers.** This crowd conducts their business from amongst a select few preferred venues. They are price-sensitive, negotiate skillfully and buy from the lowest bidder in their preferred group – not the lowest within the entire marketplace.

5. **Price Hounds.** These are the classic commoditized customers. All their buying decisions are based strictly and solely on price. They will do anything (including bluffing and outright shading the truth) to get the absolute lowest price without regard for anything else. Most Price Hounds, by definition, are not decision-makers, and the few who are tend to be so difficult to deal with you wonder if booking the event with them is even worth it.

Now before we go any further, let's take a close look at those last two buyers: Dealers and Price Hounds. There are very clear differences between a legitimate Price Negotiator (Dealer) who wants the lowest price possible without all the bells and whistles – and a Price Hound, as enumerated here:

The Price Negotiator	The Price Hound
It's a two-way street.	It's a one-way street.
It's a positive communication.	It tends to be a negative conversation, to the point of droning on and on.
It's a "win/win." There is a give and take to the conversation; you can sense it.	Its "win-lose" – all take, very little give.

THE PRICE NEGOTIATOR	THE PRICE HOUND
The information provided is candid, complete and up front; very transparent.	The information provided is incomplete, even purposefully misleading
Has a number he needs to reach and knows you have a number you must reach.	He has a number and couldn't care less about your number.
It is a friendly conversation.	It tends to be a cold, even an unfriendly, conversation, which he tries to dominate.
There is a tempo and a quickness to it, because he really does want to get to a decision to buy.	There is no tempo. It is a prolonged and dragged out encounter. If any concession is made at all, it is miniscule, and yet touted as a major give-back on his part.
He doesn't rush you.	He is almost always in a rush to "get pricing" or "get a menu kit."
He is willing to meet directly.	He avoids meeting directly as much as possible.

I would say roughly 75% to 80% of true buyers make their decisions based on trust, and about 20% to 25% do so based on price. In terms of distribution, out of 25 possible call-in customers, you should expect to have 18 or 19 buying on trust and six or seven on price, right? Regrettably, in the "real world" of sales, the breakdown is more like 15 or 16 on price, and nine or 10 – or even fewer – on trust. Why? It tends to be the nature of call-ins. Price hounds, in particular, tend to be call-ins. From their vantage point, the more salespeople they talk with, the lower the price will ultimately be. And, I must admit, they are usually correct.

Beyond very basic transactions – and by that, I mean buying gas for my car – if a gas station six blocks away is selling it for 25 cents less per gallon, that's where I'm going. If milk is $1.00 less at a particular store, I'm buying it for $1.00 less. But what about buying a house or doing major home renovations? What about buying life insurance/estate planning or buying a catered banquet event? I think it's a little bit different, don't you? Think of it this way: If buyers only purchased from the lowest priced bidder, then why do the leading caterers have higher prices? Or, to be a bit more direct about it, is your product or service really any good if people will not pay more for it?

THE ILLUSION OF SELLING

The average salesperson gets caught up in the moment of the day-to-day grind and never quite gets past the "So what are your prices?" "What's this going to cost me?" remarks. They never have that in-depth conversation about needs and some quite frankly don't think it makes any difference. To them, it is always all about dates, rates and space. They convince themselves they are selling, when in fact they are doing nothing of the kind. They are also the very first ones to say it's all about price. They like to say: "What are we willing to do, in terms of lowering the price, to get or keep the business?" And still worse, some even ask this question before they have spoken directly with the potential customer. It is all about price for them, because email and the telephone tend to be mostly reactive – a price quote, a number.

In the case of Price Hounds, what I call the "Nice Price Hounds" usually will meet with you. And, of course, they will then press you to discuss price and/or send pricing information as soon as possible. You see it all the time: many corporate and fundraising organizations make it a common practice to call three or four venues every year to secure price quotes, only to stay put in the same facility they've been using for the past 10 years. This is all done under the guise of "due diligence." When dealing with the "Not-so-nice Price Hounds," you will find they think there is absolutely no need to ever meet with you. They'll say they just don't have time. They tend to be abrupt and slightly dismissive, and they are always in a tremendous rush to have all the pricing information "yesterday." Come now, are we really to believe this conference for 200 people just came up a few hours ago, and a venue decision must be made within 24 or 48 hours? Strong salespeople have a healthy skepticism about this claim.

Still another hallmark of the "Not-so-nice Price Hound" is he likes to tell you straight out that he is collecting pricing or getting menus from "several places." This, of course, is usually nothing more than an intimidation tactic, surprisingly a very effective one with many sales-people. In this case, there is an absolute rush to secure pricing as soon as possible, yet one week later the same individual may tell you the conference has been put on hold or completely cancelled.

If your sales experience is relegated to strictly what comes in over the telephone and, more likely, email (and if you are not analyzing which type of buyer you are dealing with), then you are missing out on the most exciting, the most rewarding, the most dynamic part of selling. It's a little bit like the difference between watching television on a 24" screen and watching on a 65" high-definition plasma screen with surround sound. It's just two completely different experiences. Well, if it's not about dates, rates, space and price quotes, then what is it all about?

The First Key: It's All About Deferring

The ability to defer is one of the keys that separate the average and inex-perienced salesperson from the star performer. The skilled salesperson isn't selling food and beverage, he is selling what it will do for you. His focus is on bringing the customer closer, the average salesperson's focus is on not letting the customer get away. His approach is rooted in confi-dence, is open-minded and relaxed, not reactive, fearful and tense. The result? He develops a closer relationship and ultimately, a better sales experience for both the customer and himself.

When a customer or prospect asks you a question, it's important to try to answer it as promptly as possible. So, when you absolutely must, it's quite all right to give a very broad price range. The more sophisti-cated salesperson will, however, skillfully defer pricing questions as much as possible.

> Focus on uncovering needs and building trust
> before the price question even comes up.

Strong salespeople see Price Hounds for what they are and then purposely change the dynamics of play. They change the conversation from what the customer expects to hear to what he doesn't expect to hear. They "change it up," as we say in tennis, and refuse to be intimidated. First, they purposefully slow down the conversation, through both their tone and body language. This action alone conveys a certain calmness and self-control. They are showing they are not desperate to make a sale today and are certainly willing to walk away from this type of buyer if need be.

If it's truly all about price, then yes, the buyer should book the lowest bidder. If it's solely a price decision, then you need to let them know, "I'm really not the guy for you." With certain intimidating people, we may even want to name the competitor who does have absolutely the lowest price in the market. This goes back to having a winning mindset. Are you playing to win or are you afraid to lose? Are you acting from confidence and, thus, drawing this individual closer to you, or are you acting out of fear and trying not to lose the customer?

In the case of the "Passive-Aggressive Price Hound," overt intimidation is not their preferred method. At some point in the conversation, though, they will subtly go negative, putting down your venue or even you yourself to get you to address the price issue up front or quote your lowest price. Strong salespeople immediately stop and step in to address the remark with either a very direct comment back or a direct question challenging the person to substantiate his unfounded remarks. Confident salespeople put the Passive-Aggressive Hounds back on their heels and put the conversation back on a level playing field.

THE SECOND KEY: IT'S ALL ABOUT VALUE

What is considered "Value" to one customer can be completely different to another customer. As a salesperson, you can never assume you know what "value" means until you uncover it, prospect by prospect. It must reflect what the customer deems important. You can't decide the values a potential customer considers most important, either. Value can't be imposed on a buyer. That's why you need to listen and ask questions. And, you cannot add value until you know the customer's needs. Unthinking salespeople try to inflict on the potential customer what they "think" is of value to him or her. While you might have some idea of what a customer's values are, you cannot be certain until you verify it.

The very worst mistake so many salespeople make is to reveal the price and then try to "back into" some kind of value discussion. Conversely, when a legitimate customer sees the value of your product or service, price usually becomes a secondary issue. To establish customer value, however, the salesperson must clearly understand what their products/services offer that creates value. This goes back to one of the subcategories of the "Knowledge Habit": Know your products/services and venue as well as you know those of your competitors. If you do, your potential customer's trust level will start to rise. If you don't, you will fall back into reactive mode, and reactive always sounds like price.

> When your focus is on customer value, you have more overall control, you better direct the sales experience, and further differentiate yourself from the competition.

Where do you want to play the game? Do you want to play on price or value? Value is the sweet spot. All good tennis and golf players know what the sweet spot is. Some players call it "the zone." I like that one, too, because it speaks to me of being highly focused, yet calm. Whatever metaphor works for you is fine. In most sales situations, you will offer potential customers one or more of the following simple values:

More for the money	Detailed /Thorough	More comfort
Greater flexibility	Constructive advice	Peace of Mind

Make their life easier	Price Competitive (not lowest)	Professional
Total Honesty	Consistency	Familiarity
Make them look good	Solid & Constructive Advice	Associates perceived as helpful
Increased profit	Easy to do Business with	Enthusiasm
Positive Attitude	Reputation (both yours and your company)	Non-embarrassment

I'm sure you can think of a few others.

INDISPENSABLE VALUES

While all values are important if they are important to your customer, I recommend paying particular attention to these values:

1. Making them look good
2. Peace of mind.
3. Non-embarrassment.

These are huge, huge values, which so many overlook, forget or take for granted. When you excel at delivering on these values, your customer starts to relax. He starts to believe he can count on you. He is not worried about being embarrassed, he believes all will go well and he will receive credit from his boss for a successful event. Sell to that intangible need, sell that value first. Focus, as well, on providing constructive advice, being price competitive (not "cheapest"), being enthusiastic/hungry and – above all – being honest. It's a combination that's hard to beat and will put you in a place way out front of all your competitors. You need to emphasize these values, not the square footage of the ballroom or that you recently refurbished the ballroom – he can see all of that for himself.

"More"

"More" is a big deal in the world of sales. Don't ever take it for granted or underestimate its power. Slow down as you emphasize what makes you different and, therefore, a better choice. Linger over these differentiating points. Whenever possible, seize the opportunity to drive your point home clearly and concisely.

A few examples:

- More flexibility with deposits and due dates.
- More creative and exciting menus at a mid-level price point.
- More appropriate menu for the audience or the season or the occasion.
- More handholding.
- More detailed and thorough.

With value, the operative word will always be "More."

> When you are value-focused, you will win customer loyalty and the golden gift of referrals - the most important rewards in sales.

It's All about Pain, Too

Another effective way to sell value is to identify, and avoid, a customer's pain points. Think in terms of their entire value construct: What keeps this customer awake at night? How can I address it? How does what I offer directly address the customer's concerns? How do I articulate my offering impactfully and memorably to this customer? How do I prove it?

Common Customer Pain Points

- Miscommunications/untimely communication
- Complicating my life

- Not really listening
- Putting me in last minute situations where I do not have any other options
- Unreliable or inconsistent service or quality
- Over-promising and under-delivering
- Slow – or no – response
- Responses that invite even more questions than were asked
- Lack of empathy
- Piling on additional charges
- Hidden charges
- Lack of deadline sensitivity
- Voicemail
- Poor sales training – spotty knowledge of both products and services
- Poor attention to detail
- Lack of integrity—Shading the truth
- Aggravation
- Worry
- Negative /Reactive Attitude.

"Less"

Key into customer pain points; it is a huge component of sales. People will pay more if they are confident you will not be creating any more pain for them and/or will eliminate the pain they have experienced in the past. Too many salespeople get so caught up in their own needs (for example, "I have to make this sale!") that they don't fully listen to the customer's pain and what discomfort they have experienced.

You want your prospective customers to have pain points. If your prospect does not have a significant problem to solve – if they don't have a few pain points – then you are going to have a very difficult time getting them to fairly evaluate your venue, much less make a decision to buy from you. The operative word when talking about pain is Less. To my point: No pain, No gain.

> The very best salespeople are not selling
> products and services; they are selling Outcomes/
> Results, Solutions Pain Relief and Experiences.

FAKE VALUES

Often salespeople emphasize points or values they "think" matter to the customer. For example, their trustworthiness and integrity, or simply how much they value the customer's business and want to work with them on a collaborative basis. These are, of course, important but all too often the salesperson will start talking about these values way too early in the conversation, before he knows what's most important to this prospective customer and before he has established his own value. You can overplay these themes as your core values if you do not link them to a specific customer you have personally worked with before.

A salesperson trying to book a conference once claimed the prospective customer's key need (their "hot button" to use his jargon) was "to feel valued." This is absolute nonsense and indicative of those that play the all motion is progress game. What does that mean? It's way too vague, indicating the salesperson didn't know what he was doing. He hadn't even done the basic homework of finding out one or two of the client's real needs prior to the visit. "Feeling valued" is not a value or an end in itself. It's a result of fulfilling specific needs.

Without that emotional connection to an actual customer, your narrative will be too general, too vague; it will lack the strength it needs to compel the customer to take action. Worse yet, the customer will start to disengage from you. It all becomes "just noise" and turns them off. The same applies to such claims as, "I want to win your business" or "We share your values." You hear these catchy little phrases all the time, but it's just noise. The ineffective salesperson employs these tactics because he does not do the necessary homework ahead of time; he goes for what he thinks is the easy fix. It doesn't work. When introduced in the proper sequence in the value discussion, it can be very effective; otherwise when you lead with this, it comes across to the customer as hollow and fake.

It All Starts With Very Simple Things

When most people initially meet a salesperson, they want to get a sense of who he is, how long he has worked at this venue, and what he stands for, as well as what he knows and doesn't know. Before you can start establishing any values and any level of trust, you first have got to nail the simple things such as:

- Calling when you say you will.
- Returning phone calls promptly.
- Providing correct and complete information to all questions in a timely manner
- Being on time for appointments and respecting your customer's time schedule
- Being detailed and thorough
- Knowing the operational capabilities and logistics of the venue and each meeting space
- Looking at and listening to your prospective customer
- Answering questions without hesitating and without being evasive.

All too often, this bedrock principle in establishing a relationship (it goes right back to Chapter 1 about being authentic) is overlooked or skipped over in the rush of the day. Don't let it happen to you. You risk building trust, and without trust, all is lost.

You will find that buyers who are very knowledgeable about your services are more likely to be very value focused. They want to deal with a salesperson who is knowledgeable and trustworthy, as well. Their expectation as a customer is to be well taken care of, advised of and kept up to date on all aspects (particularly any changes) regarding their business with you. They are truly relationship buyers. They expect high value at a reasonable price. These are the customers who, over time, become your Rock Stars if you honor the relationship. As a salesperson, every interaction with them is another opportunity for you to add value and drive loyalty.

Note: At the beginning of this section I indicated customers want to know how long you have been working at this venue. That is an extremely important question – to the customer. Your answer to that question says several important things to them. Generally, the longer you have been there the better. Skillful salespeople bring this into the conversation early in the game to help further establish their value and start gaining trust.

> The customer will always:
>
> 1. Buy or not buy you first
> 2. Buy or not buy your products/services second.

THE THIRD KEY: IT'S ALL ABOUT DEEPENING THE EXPERIENCE

We talked about locking in on simple values…going for that sweet spot. Here is where the best really excel. They step up their game even more because they are playing the game above the fray. Strong salespeople always bring more to the sales experience than do their counterparts. As much as we sell outcomes and solutions to problems, the best transform their interactions with customers and their events into "memorable experiences." Strong salespeople always have a good sense of the values they themselves personally bring to the marketplace, and an especially good sense of the values in which their companies excel. They demonstrate a strong service attitude (which, hard to believe, can occasionally be lacking in the hospitality industry), and they are focused on how they can provide not just good or acceptable, but outstanding service to their customers.

A strong and sincere service attitude, coupled with a commitment to providing outstanding service – this is what differentiates the sales experience for the customer. It is a huge value that is easy to take for granted. It aids you, though, immeasurably in building trust and loyalty. It paints you as an individual of high integrity who is proud of what he does for a living – a very appealing, and winning, combination. In this regard:

GO DEEPER

Check those below that you can confidently say you consistently do to deepen the customer's positive experience:

Do I have seasonal menus? Do I have the executive chef attend and engage our customers at tastings? Is our culinary service staff knowledgeable and experienced?

Do I earn customer loyalty by offering superior quality/service?

Do I take the hassle out of buying?

Do I really focus on and uncover the purpose of each event?

Do I sell the long-term advantages of our products and services?

Do I take advantage of all the free education my company offers? It makes me a better, more knowledgeable salesperson and, therefore, a better value to our customers.

Do I explain? The best salespeople are always educating their customers and, in so doing build loyalty.

Do I find new ways to help clients solve problems, grow revenue, cut costs and reduce risk?

Do I build in upgrades? It differentiates you from the competition and sets the stage for better overall pricing.

Do I perform in ways that make the client look good?

Do I consciously and methodically discover the customer's values? Do I also discover the customer's pain points – both past and present?

Am I their "go-to person"? If a customer has a problem with one of my venue's policies, do I just step back, or do I get involved and solve the problem? If you get involved, I can assure you your customers think of you as their "go-to person," and they also refer you to their friends and associates.

Do I stay current with catering trends? New technologies? New food and beverages? Customers might not say it directly, but they could very well be thinking your offerings are out of date, stale or just too plain.

Do I make customers wait too long while discussing an issue with internal peers? Customers want their interaction with you to be quick and decisive. Don't let them think you are not in charge. The longer you make them wait, the more that seed of doubt has a chance to grow.

Am I an authority? Pick a specific market or type of an event and learn as much about it as possible. Become the go-to person within your company and your network.

Do I intelligently articulate my company's culture and how it aligns with my client's corporate culture and mission statement?

Do I patiently allow customers to make all sorts of changes and/or repeatedly go over specific details again and again until they are comfortable? Do I do this without reflecting any irritation whatsoever?

Do I stay in touch with prospects and customers, even when there is no immediate need for our services? The very best salespeople connect with prospective customers regularly, before their services are needed. This is a critical differentiator.

How many check marks did you have?

- *Fortune* Magazine debuted in 1929 right after the Great Wall Street Crash. They were charging $1.00 per issue. By comparison; the *New York Times* Sunday edition was selling at five cents per issue. Circulation of *Fortune* grew from 30,000 in 1929 to 460,000 in 1937 during the worst financial collapse this country has ever experienced.[36]
- When Disneyland opened in 1955, the industry consensus was that it would be an absolute failure. But Disney wasn't selling an amusement park; he was offering a family park where parents and children could have fun together. Disney put it this way:

"We are selling happiness."[37]

Disney didn't go into this venture with just the idea of making money. Making money was, of course, important, but it came as a result of focusing on making families happy first.

Now, this will sound totally contradictory to what I have been preaching, however indispensable salespeople stand out from the crowd in difficult economic times. They change things up big time. As much as they know it is important to maintain price points, they are equally sensitive to a customer's need for flexibility when confronted with either a major economic downturn effecting the entire economy, or a similarly catastrophic situation limited to their company or industry. Thankfully, these kinds of dramatic business downturns occur only about once every 10 to 15 years. The more personally devastating situations occur at random. They can be very challenging to navigate and, when they do occur, all are taken by surprise. This is an area where that sense of touch we spoke about very much comes into play.

While many salespeople have a narrower focus and are fixated on

---

[36] *Hope: How Triumphant Leaders Create the Future* by Andrew Razeghi, John Wiley & Sons Publishing

[37] *How to Be Like Walt: Capturing the Disney Magic Every Day of Your Life*, by Pat Williams, Health Communications, Inc., 2004.

making sure they get what they are owed and what was contracted for in writing, indispensable salespeople are busy going in the exact opposite direction. They are busy being as flexible as possible and working together with the customer as a true partner to achieve a workable solution for both parties. They know that once they have planted the seed, they will reap the rewards of customer loyalty, referrals and repeat business when the economy rebounds, as it always does. This is how you not only deepen the experience but the relationship. This is why – over the long term – indispensable salespeople always have a much more extensive and deeper account base of repeat business than do their counterparts. Loyalty will always be a salesperson's long-range key profit driver.

In its most simplistic form, you need to think and act regarding value and price in four ways:

1. **Communicate.** Clearly set forth values first, then show price. Great salespeople take customers who are initially totally price-focused and bring them to a level where they are equally if not more value-focused. The very last thing you ever want to talk about is price.

2. **Educate.** Having low prices is remembered less often than having low quality. When you compete exclusively on price, you might very well secure the business, but you usually also secure more complaints when the event takes place, and more disputes on billing, as well as few, if any referrals. Rather than discount, differentiate your venue from cheaper alternatives and educate your customers as to what those differences really are.

3. **Simplify.** When a person asks about a discount, many times it simply reflects confusion about your specific proposal and/or all the other options in the marketplace to be considered. If you explain how you determined your price and if you have a

rational pricing structure, it will make sense to the customer. Keep it simple and you will always be in great scoring position.

4. **Verify.** When confronted with the comment, "You are more expensive than several other venues," verify exactly what is included in each competitor's price. Review the pricing line by line to verify you are comparing apples to apples. If you have offered a rational price package, more often than not you will find there are differences in what exactly is included in the competing price quote.

Too often, inexperienced salespeople are flustered in this discussion of pricing and jump to conclusions – wrong conclusions. They fall into the trap of trying to compete with an invalid offer. They fall into playing defense at the exact moment they need to be on offense.

RAISE YOUR GAME

True sales professionals in major companies compete on execution. They focus on being the best in execution and worry much less about being cheaper. The best caterers focus on superior service and creative food presentations. They key into deepening the experience, reliability and – just as important – their own knowledge and personal experience.

No matter how basic the event, there will always be non-price aspects, and these always matter to customers. It is your responsibility – through discussion, questions, logic, vivid examples and real stories – to remind prospective customers of those aspects and how you can best address them. Customer relationships are built upon and grow through differentiation and the salesperson's willingness to contribute more beyond the basics of what is expected.

> When told a competitor is "cheaper," true sales professionals raise their game and speak to how they are better.

In upcoming chapters we'll discuss prospecting, solicitation and networking – all of which expose you to a much broader universe of individuals who are much less price driven, much more quality driven and much more relationship driven. Although they may not always be the true decision makers, these contacts are usually important and valuable influencers.

TAKEAWAYS:

*We are in the business of raising relationships,
not necessarily lowering pricing.*

You sell value by first proving your own value.

*If you are not creating value, you are
probably not creating profit either.*

*Next time someone asks, "What's the price?" rephrase the
question in your mind to, "Is there value in this?"*

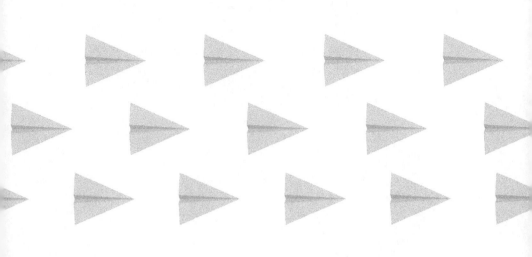

SECTION 2

THE DAILY DRILL

"Do not go where the path may lead; go instead where there is no path and leave a trail."[38] *– Ralph Waldo Emerson*

---

[38] EverydayPower.com

CHAPTER 4

Prospecting

Prospecting is the first in a two-step process called "Solicitation." Prospecting initiates the entire solicitation process. While most perceive prospecting as tedious work, when executed correctly, prospecting is a highly strategic activity.

Great prospectors have well-defined organizational skills. They quickly evaluate a large amount of data and then synthesize that information into priority order. This upfront research, coupled with generally strong, effective sales skills and a persistent determination to prospect on a regular basis, leads to higher closing ratios.

Prospecting and solicitation are analogous to many sports, including tennis. Strong tennis players are quick on their feet and have great balance. They are always on their toes, shift quickly and respond even quicker. Their focus is forward-thinking, anticipatory and positive. Reactive players tend to be flat footed, not fully engaged and passive. Although they often get the ball back across the net, they hit defensive shots and certainly don't move things forward or quickly win points. The proactive player moves with the ball, whereas the reactive player waits to see where the ball is going. In the first case, you are in the game; in the second, you're late to the game. Wayne Gretzky (of the New York Rangers) said it best:

> **"A good hockey player plays where the puck is. A great hockey player plays where the puck is going to be."[39]**

---

[39] Brainyquote.com

The Fear Factor

In their book *The Psychology of Sales Call Reluctance,*[40] George Dudley's and Shannon Goodson's research shows that as many as 80% of new salespeople fail in their first year due to insufficient prospecting. Similarly, at some points in their careers more than 40% of veteran salespeople do not sufficiently prospect. Why? Fear of failure. The salesperson's own inner voice predicts a negative reaction, which prevents him from picking up the telephone or sending a letter of introduction. The fallback is they reactively respond to the usual telephone or email inquiry, but if you call this prospecting, you are only fooling yourself. There is a lot of talk about prospecting but, when you get right down to it, there is much less actual prospecting going on than you would think.

The Prospecting Spectrum

On one end of the prospecting spectrum we have unskilled and inexperienced salespeople and, as you might suspect, they absolutely loathe prospecting and, by extension, actual solicitation. They abhor it so much you can actually see their backs arch when the subject comes up. These individuals thrive instead on mind-numbing reactive routine. If they suspect an inquiry may be even a little bit outside their ideal norm, they find a way to avoid it or turn it away. In their world, the illusion they allow themselves is that just about every group they are already working with will rebook. There's no need, therefore, to get further bogged down with this sort of needless prospecting stuff – or so they think. The usual excuses offered are:

- "Besides, we are too busy with what is happening right now."
- "Besides, we can't keep up with all the inquiries coming in over the phone already!"
- "Besides, there is so little available meeting space to sell anyway!"

---

[40] Published by Behavioral Sciences Research Press, Inc., 2007.

Yes, ineffective salespeople have innumerable excuses/rationalizations for not prospecting for new business. They are quite satisfied with the status quo. Of course, however, not everything rebooks, and companies/organizations all go through their own ups and downs, cutbacks and restructurings. These salespeople are usually puzzled (actually, startled) when an account does not rebook. When the floor falls out from under them, they go into full panic mode ("The sky is falling!") and their desperation is quite evident to all.

On the very opposite end of the spectrum are those relatively few well-intentioned proactive prospectors. Regrettably, some of these individuals make the mistake of setting the bar too low in determining from whom they will solicit. If you set out to prospect everyone, you will end up prospecting no one. These folks make the critical mistake of going after people who, for one reason or another, are either unable or unwilling to buy.

In the very middle of the prospecting range, however, are those strong proactive salespeople. When the business environment shifts, they don't panic at all because they have options. These indispensable performers very calmly and methodically move from one prospecting option to the next. They inherently understand the need to *continually prospect* for new business. They lead their teams in this area by the power of their example and their innate ability to zone in on "what appear to be...."

LIKELY PROSPECTS

When it comes to prospecting, your role models should be commissioned salespeople, entrepreneurs, and many immigrants and small business owners. All these people have a huge advantage over those who work for corporations. They clearly understand that if they don't make a sale, they don't eat. Therefore, they carefully prioritize their prospects and sales activities by the "likelihood of close." It's really that simple. Even more important, they are ruthlessly honest with themselves so they can quickly and effectively engage potential prospects, execute actions and always keep moving forward – closer to a sale.

Your goal, therefore – if you are honest – must be to spend most of your valuable time with likely prospects. Peak performers confront themselves daily with such questions as: "What organizations or companies with real potential am I targeting this week?" and "Is the individual I just spoke with today really a likely prospect for me?" The same principle applies as in Chapter 3 where we asked you to think about where you want to play the game: On value or on price? Here, the question is do you want to play the game with likely or unlikely prospects? It does take a little more time to sift through/identify who are most likely and ready to become your next customers, but it is time well spent.

Top performers are always in the hunt. They are always focused on "likely prospects." With truly engaged salespeople, it is always about today, about now. Ineffective salespeople, on the other hand, are very much about yesterday or some vague "tomorrow." There is a lot of "I think so…" or "Could be…" in their day. However, it really all comes down to these three little questions:

1. Does this person buy, need or want *exactly* what I am selling?
2. Is this person showing some *real* interest in possibly buying from me?
3. Can this person afford to host the event with us? Does he/she have the money?

Note: These three questions apply to the entire solicitation process. In the prospecting phase specifically, you will focus on answering questions #1 and #3. You would not be able to address Question #2 until you have spoken directly with the prospect on your follow-up call. Now, let's review some of the more common situations that take place in the everyday world of sales.

THE "RIGHT IN FRONT OF YOU" PROSPECTS

I have been appalled to discover catering salespeople who handle major annual conferences for some of the very largest blue-chip corporations, and yet just don't seem to know the full extent of the other local catering events the corporation does in their own city. For example, a major consumer products company holds an annual holiday party for 2,400 people, or a major pharmaceuticals company hosts two annual local holiday parties for 1,000 people each. In both cases, the salespeople already handled major annual conferences for the organizations, and yet they were totally unaware of these other large events. For whatever reason, they just could not take the time to ask their clients a few simple questions, such as:

- What other events does your company host?
- Are there any other event planners in your organization you would suggest I contact?

Or the most basic:

- Who plans your company's annual holiday party?

It all goes back to having a curious mind and being knowledgeable. It speaks to being forward thinking and on your toes. Yes, it goes back to those essential habits we have reviewed.

THE HOT PROSPECTS?

A national sales leader sent an email about a "phenomenal prospect" one of his salespeople had come across. The only thing "standing in the way" were two local/social catering events on hold for the largest ballroom. Contracts had been sent for the latter events, but were not yet signed. The immediate directive was to notify the groups in question and find alternate dates for them, if possible. The "phenomenal" prospect needed to know our availability today and required a full proposal by Monday. A final decision, we were told, would be made on Tuesday. I started to instinctively get the feeling we were embarking on an "all motion is progress" caper.

Sure enough, after notifying both groups, Tuesday came and went without a word from the "phenomenal" prospect. Radio silence ensued all day Wednesday, as well. Finally, on Thursday we were notified (again by email), but this time by the sales manager, not the national sales leader, that our venue and even our city were ruled out because, unfortunately, our room rates were just too high. We were thanked profusely for all our assistance in this "team effort," and the note even ended with one of those happy faces with the smile turned upside down. Got it – you're disappointed. It turns out the sales manager had only one brief telephone conversation with the prospective customer; the rest of their communication was by email. The sales manager was inexperienced, lacked strong selling and prospecting skills, didn't qualify the lead and, consequently, totally misjudged it.

Every lead is a strong lead to a new sales manager because they just don't know how to differentiate. Most do little if any legitimate prospecting. They simply respond (react) to emails. To be blunt, these individuals (at least at this stage of their careers) are not salespeople, they are order takers. While I can understand the sales manager's excitement, what's the sales leader's excuse? This was a classic case of a "very strong prospect" right up until it wasn't.

Here's another example, from a slightly different prospective. This salesperson had a history of having initially "very strong" leads. He felt this piece of business was quite strong and wanted to set up a tasting with the potential client to show him exactly what we could do for them. Based on my suspicions and experience with this salesperson, I decided not to attend the tasting which, I suspected, would morph into an "all motion is progress" swirl.

The potential customer came in for the tasting with our executive chef. Several key executives from the venue attended, as well. As a follow up, the salesperson emailed me, the other executives and the general manager, regaling us with how happy and impressed the potential customer was with the tasting. Being supportive managers, we all sent back encouraging emails saying we hoped the event moved forward and booked.

One week went by – no word. After two weeks (a long time in our business), I asked the salesperson for a status update on the booking, which most others had completely forgotten about by now. The startled salesperson responded that as much as the potential customer loved the food and loved the presentation, it was just too expensive for them, so they were going to book the event at a local college.

Wow! What a waste of money! More important, what a colossal waste of time – senior leadership's time, the executive chef's time and, most important, the salesperson's time. And when you really think about it, what an erosion of the salesperson's own goodwill and credibility with the executive committee members who did attend the tasting.

REALITY CHECK

Let's go back to the basics. In these examples, *ask yourself:*

> - Where was the qualification?
> - Where was the laser focus on qualifying and, by extension, actually booking the events?
> - Was there ever any focus on being honest with ourselves, let alone the potential customer, about each piece of business?

All motion is not progress. Wasn't there a certain amount of deception going on here? If the customer doesn't have the necessary budget, no matter how good the food is, he will not be booking the event. In the first example, if the organization doesn't have the money, they will not be staying in New York City hotels – the most expensive in the country. Whether self-deception or outright deception, good salespeople avoid it. They know it demeans them and their profession and takes the focus away from real sales opportunities.

THE PROSPECTING PROCESS

Prospecting is more an attitude than anything else – a "searching" attitude that is always open to discovering new relationships and new business opportunities to aggressively pursue. Can that attitude be learned/developed? To a degree, yes, but the essential curiosity must be there from the start.

The overarching goal of prospecting is to connect to a legitimate buyer. For our purposes, a legitimate buyer is someone (as noted earlier) who buys, needs or wants exactly what I am selling, who shows some real interest in buying from me and, most important, can afford to buy from me. Pretty simple. In the prospecting phase, you'll want to qualify each lead to see how closely each measures up to this criteria before committing yourself any further to the sales process.

I like to call all opportunities, inquiries, call-ins, emails, prospects, etc., "Leads." Very simple. And just like police detectives, salespeople encounter all sorts of leads and outright reject many of them. Upon closer inspection and research, we reject even more. The few that survive are upgraded to "Prospects." Now the probing and research begins, leading to telephone follow up and, conceivably, a face-to-face meeting with the prospective customer. If ever it was important to be ruthlessly honest with ourselves, this is it.

The process of prospecting is fairly easy; it is the process of preparation. There are three parts to the process. Let's take them one at a time:

1. Sources. For a good prospector, sources are unlimited; you just need to look. Specifically, you need to look with an open mind at all those wonderful possibilities surrounding you. Don't censor yourself. Mailing lists, local and national newspapers, college alumni directories – even your own company's annual report – are great source material. On a regular basis, be sure to attend trade shows, chamber of commerce events, bridal fairs, and events hosted by professional and community philanthropic organizations. Talking with convention and visitors' bureaus and destination management companies provides you with even more opportunities. And, don't overlook referrals from customers and vendors, as well as reviewing old lost business reports. Of course, search engines, such as Google, MSN, LinkedIn, Hoovers, Spokeo and Biznik also come into play.

During this phase, you will also want to look out for new and growing companies, industries and sectors of the economy, as well as recession-resistant organizations. As of this printing, Amazon and Apple would qualify as growing companies. Pharmaceuticals, health-care and senior-related industries would certainly be growing sectors of the economy as the huge baby boomer demographic enters retirement. The emerging markets of Asia (specifically China and India), as well as Russia, present major opportunities, especially if your venue is in a large city with a very diverse population. The same applies to African American and Hispanic communities – all present huge opportunities to develop a wide variety of both business and personal events.

2. Research. Next, do some quick research on your sources. "Google" them to get a better sense of each organization. See who is on the executive board/staff and do some quick pre-qualifying. Look for names with the title of Director of Development, Director of Meetings and Conferences, Vice President of Development, Executive Director or Director of Human Resources. You want decision-makers/influencers. Avoid such titles as Special Events Coordinator, Office Manager or Director of Purchasing. You do need to be nice to them – one day they may be decision-makers – but they are not your key audience today. Also look for the company or organization's mission statement (scour their website, journal or annual report), and uncover some history as to where they have done past events and the scope of those events. This information alone can give you an indication as to whether this group will be open to considering your venue. Once you have whittled down your sources through research, it's time for the initial pre-qualification, or prioritization, process. As a result, some will be promoted to key prospects, while others will fall by the wayside. Still others will fall somewhere in between.

I mentioned earlier in this chapter the idea of "likely prospects." What are they: Organizations that are already hosting events. What *aren't* they: Organizations that have hosted an event for 25 years at the same very small exclusive boutique hotel in a very wealthy area of the city would not be a likely prospect for a large convention type of venue located in the midtown business district.The same holds true for events that have a very long history at one facility or have traditionally booked in suburban versus urban centers. These are not likely prospects, unless there are extenuating circumstances (e.g., the event is doubling in size this year or needs a more centrally located venue).

The Prospecting Funnel. Many readers, I am sure, are familiar with the term "Prospecting Funnel." The basic idea is excellent – the more leads you place in the top of the funnel, the more you will net at the bottom. Here's the catch: Unsuccessful salespeople like to lie to themselves (remember "the illusion of selling"?) by indiscriminately filling the top of the funnel with all sorts of leads – good, bad and indifferent. Their focus is on "seeing what will stick," as they say. In addition, they think they will sound really busy when asked to report-out on their sales initiatives. Great salespeople like to put lots of leads in the funnel, too, but they make a distinction between the very vague "potential "prospects and those all-important "likely prospects."

You can go badly off track if you succumb to quantifying/measuring sales by the number of prospects you have in your sales funnel. These processes suck the life out of sales. A professional golfer selects the club he thinks will most effectively get him where he needs to be at any moment on the course. A skilled tennis player will make a shot selection based on his opponent's movement on the court and what he thinks will result in a winning point. The same is true of great salespeople; they add legitimate leads to the funnel that have real potential to result in real sales. Based on that criteria (and using my golf analogy), because of their confidence in both the lead and their own skill as salespeople, they aim and expect (with their next offensive shot) to put that ball right on the green and in good scoring position.

On the same note, at one of my former companies, any time a salesperson did anything on an account, it was logged in as an "activity." Invariably, two or three times a year the entire sales force would get a memo from someone in corporate enlisting his/her support to generate more activities. The memo would always have some cutesy artwork stating in bold letters: "It's all about the activity!" Again, all this plays right into that same "all motion is progress" charade. If all you do is measure activities or number of prospects, then that is all you will get – a number. You must pick and choose your activities and your prospects.

Good salespeople know it is neither about activities nor loading up the funnel; it's all about closing business.

3. Establishing the Contact. The next step: Call and find out who oversees planning the event you are focusing on and/or verify the name you believe to be the person in charge. In most cases, people will gladly give you (or verify for you) the name and title of the person in charge of planning the event. But as is human nature, you will occasionally get a few people who may not want to give you the information you need. It's not personal; these are what I call the "speed bumps" you can expect along the way, such as:

Speed Bumps

"Oh, we are already set for this year."

My response: "Actually, I was calling about next year; who might that person be who is in charge?"

"We are very happy with X venue."

My response: "Of course I can understand that and certainly respect that. At the same time, don't you think your company shouldn't ignore the possibility that we might very well be an even better alternative? For no other reason, if the venue you currently use were completely booked the next time you called, what would be your fallback? Don't you think you should have a second high-quality option?"

You might think my responses are a bit abrasive; I don't think they are. They are very helpful in breaking through the barriers that can momentarily stand in your way of moving forward. In a rather direct way, they nudge the person on the other end of the telephone back to the original question. Throughout, keep a positive mental attitude and a smile; a smile actually translates over the phone. You will come across as positive and professional, versus needy, self-centered or teetering on desperation.

Note: More salespeople are defeated by the "We are happy with our current venue" rationalization than by any other objection, including price.

Why did I say I am sorry though? Because it takes some of the tension out of the air. Most people answering your initial call are subjected to all sorts of demands and pressure. Rarely does someone say to them "I am sorry." By doing so, you take the pressure off. It allows them to recover, to save face and say "Ok, of course, here is the name." Be careful though; I have seen too many slick salespeople say "I'm sorry" repeatedly. Say it more than once and you sound insincere and manipulative – and you are, and it shows.

A question that often comes up is, "How can I be sure the name they give me is really the right person?" Well, you can never be 100% sure, but the title generally confirms he or she is the correct person. If someone says the title is office manager or special events coordinator I simply say, "Doesn't that person report to a director or vice president of events/conferences or development?" The answer to that question usually guides you to the right person.

The key words in the prospecting phase are "in the mail." We don't want to talk to anybody, we don't want to bother anybody. Today, our goal is simply to get a letter or an e-mail to the right person.

The sheer repetition of the follow-up calls and the variety of responses you will encounter (the speed bumps) and your responses back – all of this will help you become better and more comfortable with the process. In turn, you will sound more natural. Just like an athlete grooving his muscles, you become more and more comfortable with your scripted responses. Less is not more when it comes to prospecting.

The end game? You can't fail at prospecting unless you fail to prospect. Reggie Jackson struck out 2,597 times but he also hit 563 home runs. His short-term failure lead to his long-term success. I think Michael Jordan said it all pretty succinctly:

"I've missed more than 9,000 shots in my career. I've lost almost 300 games. Twenty-six times, I've been trusted to take the game-winning shot and missed. I've failed over and over and over again in my life, and that is why I succeed."[41]

Giving a name is easy; asking to speak to the person is little bit harder. We will get into that next.

---

[41] Brainyquote.com

Takeways:

Don't waste your time "trying to sell" to non-prospects. *You'll try too hard to make something happen too soon and usually with someone too removed from decision-making authority.*

Good prospectors have the mental edge. *They are positive they have something of value to offer a legitimate prospect. They believe the prospect is lucky I am calling today because I am going to solve a problem, show them a better way to do things and/or make their lives a little bit easier in some way.*

Poor Prospectors have a mental deficit. *They feel they are asking — actually, begging — versus offering something, and it shows.*

For indispensable performers it's always about making something happen. *For ineffective salespeople it's always about that very vague: "Well, something will happen; it always does."*

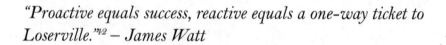

"Proactive equals success, reactive equals a one-way ticket to Loserville."[42] *– James Watt*

---

[42] *Business for Punks: Break All the Rules – The Brewdog Way,* by James Watt. Portfolio/Penguin, an imprint of Penguin Random House LLC.

CHAPTER 5

Solicitation

Prospecting and soliciting are two different animals. While prospecting is research-based, solicitation is action-based. The essential tools of solicitation correlate with the basic habit of "Connecting," and with the pillar of "Listening...then Questioning."

> Solicitation begins after you have prospected a large number of credible leads and ends with your first in-depth conversation with a potential buyer.

The critical words are "first in-depth conversation with...." Let's be frank – only losers send emails or leave voicemails and call it "solicitation." You must speak with them, too! You must get out from behind the veil of electronic communication and actually start talking with people. If you have not spoken with a potential customer, then you have not solicited them. This should be self-evident. Great salespeople find email generally lacking and, specifically as it relates to solicitation, very lacking. They see it as nothing but a crutch for the mediocre salesperson.

Great solicitors are persistent by nature, even relentless when appropriate. If these two words do not apply to you then you will never enjoy much success in sales. The best fully embrace the idea of what persistence is: A continuous course of action despite difficulties and/or opposition. And remember, every solicitation is an investment in time, and great solicitors are keenly aware that time is money. You must decide quickly how much time to spend on each solicitation. You are in charge. You own all your successes, and you also own all your failures. This is an important concept and, for the best salespeople, a huge motivator.

ADAPT OR DIE

Salespeople who make more solicitation calls book more business than those who don't, but it's not only because, statistically, making more calls increases your chances of success. Much more important: Through the very act of making all these calls, the proactive salesperson puts himself on a learning track that pays huge dividends.

> The Proactive Solicitor...
>
> ...finds out sooner what works and what doesn't.
>
> ...is faster to learn techniques that overcome/bypass potential or direct objections/rejection.
>
> ...learns more quickly how to effectively evaluate/ pre-qualify potential business and either move forward to the next step or end the solicitation entirely.
>
> ...develops self-discipline, focus and an instinctive sense for what are and are not strong leads.

Through this repetitive process, strong salespeople ultimately succeed because they learn to adapt, just as entrepreneurs, immigrants and small business owners do. For average salespeople, this is hardly ever even on their radar. The best salespeople are always in prospecting and soliciting mode. They operate with a hunter mindset. Like sharks, they must keep moving or die.

A consistent devotion to solicitation develops this "going for the jugular" instinct. Do you think that's a bit of an overstatement? The word solicitation can sound like a very nice, professional, corporate word. Bottom line, though, you are going out into the marketplace and your intention is to take a piece of business from one of your competitors. Of necessity, there is a certain intensity and drive involved to pull that off.

Qualify Quickly

When I would question some salespeople about their solicitations (for example, "Where is the organization currently hosting their event?), many times, the responses I heard back were so vague. For example: "I have to check my notes," or, "They wouldn't say." My next question always was: "Did you ask them?" More often than not, the answer was "No." On the few occasions when the answer was yes, I found they asked in an email and the prospect had not responded yet. Don't fall into the trap of thinking that emailing is talking to a person – it is not. When approached this impersonally, the customer has every reason to believe there is no need to get back to you. It can, however, look good on the salesperson's weekly sales report, because he can point to a lot of "activities." Not to over generalize, but the vast number of "also ran" salespeople seem to be quite proficient in filling out their weekly sales reports with all sorts of activities. But as we've said, "activities" do not equal sales. Speaking directly to the customer in the very beginning changes this dynamic entirely and is more likely to generate a meaningful response.

Even after the fact – after the solicitation does not pan out – I have asked: "Where did they end up booking the event? What reason did they give for not looking at us or not going with us?" – to no avail. You need to know. It is important.

Good and Bad Solicitations

I believe you can learn just as much if not more from poor solicitation examples as you can from good ones. So, let's start our discussion with what *not* to do before we get into what to do.

Email Solicitation Letter Number 1

(from a hotel administrator to the company's regional director of facility management):

> ### November 3
>
> *Hi Bob. We are trying to drum up some much-needed holiday business in catering sales. Can you please send me a list of companies that we work with on a regular basis?* **ANY CONNECTION** *that you can think of would be appreciated. Anything that you can think of would be appreciated.*

Okay, the idea was good, but the note was sent on November 3. The root cause of the problem was poor planning and execution of an intelligent solicitation effort to book holiday parties nine to 12 months prior... not four weeks prior. Most large companies set up their holiday parties at least six to nine months in advance. If anything, on November 3, we should, wherever possible, be sending internal notes to up-sell our holiday parties so we can capture as much additional revenue as possible. However, in this example, the emphasis was on looking good to internal management versus selling anything. It sounds great to say "We reached out to every single one of our vendors! We did not leave any rock unturned in our drive to secure new business!" This person conveniently never mentioned the ROI on this "Hail Mary" solicitation drive, nor that it was carried out one month in advance of the hoped-for bookings. In my opinion, too little, too late and it all plays right into that "illusion of selling" I spoke about. By the way; the ROI on the November 3 solicitation was zero.

Email Solicitation Letter Number 2:

> *Dear Jennifer:*
>
> *"I hope that you are doing well! Just a quick note to follow up my voicemail message from a few minutes ago! I*

understand your organization hosts an annual conference! For your convenience, provided above is a link to our latest e-brochure to forward to your colleagues. We would be honored to host any events that you may be planning. I would love to discuss the possibility of hosting your event.

"The XXX Venue sparkles with newly renovated rooms. Famous for its renowned XXX service, our venue is ideal for meetings and events, large and small. Planners find our venue to be perfect for corporate meetings, conventions and social events, with creative catering and impeccable service in surroundings second to none.

"Our venue has been the annual site for such prestigious events as the (names six major fundraising galas), to name a few.

"I would like to cordially invite you and your colleagues for a site visit at any time you are available. We have over xxx-amount of meeting and event space.

"I look forward to working with you and your colleagues on your upcoming program. I will call you within 10 minutes to check on your event needs. In the meantime, please contact me when I can be of assistance."

Many would say this is a strong letter and I agree, in part. There are several good things about the correspondence. However; all the good in this letter is obscured by the fact that way too much information is offered and way too soon. Let's analyze it:

- Using exclamation points in the opening sentences when there is no basis for them. Why? What is so astounding? It conveys nervousness and lack of confidence. What's worse, it expresses a certain presumption that is neither appropriate nor called for at this very preliminary stage.

- **"I hope you are doing well!"** Based on your note, you do not even know this person. So why imply that you do? This goes to being authentic in all you say and do, to start building trust.

- **"Following up on a voicemail message from a few minutes ago?"** Why not just wait until you have spoken with them or at least wait 24 hours before sending this note? It comes across as too eager and even a little strange or slightly aggressive.

- **"...provided above is a link to our latest e-brochure."** Is there a place for this in the letter? Possibly. Should it be in the second sentence? No. Why? You are giving them work to do before you've even spoken to them. Plus, you go on to describe most of the facilities anyway in your letter.

- **"We would be honored to host...."** Way too soon. If anything, you need to convey a certain sense of impartiality and reserve at this stage.

- **"...any events that you may be planning...."** Too general. You already referenced in the first sentence they have an annual conference, so why not just stay on point? Confusing.

- **"I would love to discuss...."** A professional would say something along the lines of "Thank you for your interest in our facility. I would welcome the opportunity to meet with you for a further discussion of your needs for this event."

- Paragraphs two through four are full of the usual self-serving buzzwords and inflated promotional venue descriptions.

- **"...perfect venue for a corporate meeting, convention and social events."** It is a corporate meeting as noted in their original email. Stay on point. You are showing you are neither thinking nor personalizing your note around what the customer has communicated to you.

- **"...impeccable service in surroundings second to none."** If you were selling a five-star luxury boutique venue this would apply. Otherwise, people just don't buy it.

- The six major fundraising events named in the third paragraph – though in some ways a good idea – do not relate back to this customer, who is planning a corporate event. And is now the right time to mention this? It's hard to say. It would generally be far more effective if sent after a meeting and with a formal proposal.

- As far as **"anytime you are available."** You mean you don't have a life or other clients? Wouldn't something along the lines of "at a time that is mutually convenient for all concerned" be more appropriate and professional? If nothing else, you are implying you are so eager you will do almost anything to get their business, including quickly dropping on price if they agree to meet. That's the real message being communicated.

- The last three sentences of this letter are very odd, confusing and weak. First, **"I look forward to working with you."** You have not earned the right to say this. It further points to a huge assumption on your part. Second, **"I will call you within 10 minutes"**? Again, you run the risk of appearing too eager and that is never good in sales. Third, the last sentence – **"Please contact me when I can be of assistance"** negates the previous sentence. Very confusing and, I'm sure, odd-sounding to the prospect.

I think this letter points to fear. The salesperson decided to forego speaking directly by telephone and instead did what was most comfortable for him – send information. This is the same individual who (when he does meet with a customer), comes armed with brochures, floor plans and menu kits. He would rather talk about things like floor plans than about needs. His focus seems to be more on doing things than simply being in the moment with his guest.

Despite these criticisms, many salespeople use the approach outlined in this letter. These salespeople are "hoping" the prospect books with them because they have been so nice and cheerful and given them so much information. You must develop a sense of timing as to when and where to provide different pieces of information. Is the customer ready to receive and – more important – understand all the information being sent? In most cases, the answer would be no. Less would be so much more in the illustration just referenced. Less scattered and more precise and concise would be a better way to go.

SPEED TO MARKET

The concept of speed to market gets hijacked by poor salespeople to mean getting back as "quickly" as possible; in other words no time to find out if this is even a legitimate prospect, no time to talk with them first, basically, no time to do it right. "Speed to market" is the all-purpose Band-Aid, the all-encompassing cover story, and it fits the "all motion is progress" charade perfectly. The "speed to market/ no time" defense is just a mirage – an excuse for salespeople who are unable or unwilling to ask pre-qualifying questions. They refuse to be ruthlessly honest with themselves.

Administrators, on the other hand, love that the sales manager has provided a link to their website. They admire how the manager has painted such a descriptive picture of the venue. I am not necessarily opposed to providing the potential customer with all this information; it's usually more a matter of "when" than "if." With a fully qualified prospect, at the appropriate time, "presenting" photos, etc., can be very impactful. In my experience, however, salespeople who excel in providing links and photos right out of the gate often cannot seem to close any business. They just can't seem to make it happen.

EMAIL SOLICITATION LETTER NUMBER 3:

Thank you for taking the time to review this email. I wanted to reach out to XX to see if your sales team was using mobile devices or had any plans to deploy them in the coming months. The company I represent, XX, helps sales teams be more effective with mobile devices, increasing responsiveness to customers, boosting margins and maintaining competitiveness. Would you be the correct sales leadership contact at XX to discuss this with? If you are not, any direction you could provide would be greatly appreciated.

If you're not the correct audience, I apologize. Please let me know and I'll be sure to adjust my contacts. If you'd like to review a little bit more about XX before we connect, please click here to access a brief overview.

Let's review:

- A strong solicitor would never ask if I am the correct person; he would know.
- A strong salesperson does not apologize in their very first contact with you; it comes across as weak and annoying.
- In the body of the letter I am given work to do, and I don't even know this guy!
- The solicit letter ends without a clear sense of the next action. Will the salesperson call me, or will I call him? Again, annoying.

REPLY TO AN EMAIL INQUIRY:

Hi…. It is great to hear from you. It's been awhile. Thank you for considering our venue for your upcoming program. I need to have some other details:

- *What time will you need the catering space? Is it an all-day program?*

- *Are you flexible with the dates? Can it only be in May? What are the target dates?*
- *Will you need any breakout meeting rooms?*
- *Are you only considering weekdays? Can it be a Saturday or Sunday?*
- *Is it a one-day program?*
- *What type of program is it?*
- *Will you need a separate room for lunch?*
- *How will you need it to be set?*
- *How many people are you expecting?*
- *Is there a budget you are working with?*
- *Will there be food and beverage? Will alcohol be served?*
- *Are you looking at other venues at this point?*
- *Is this an annual event?*
- *Is there a website where I can learn more about your organization?*
- *Has this event taken place before and if so where?*

I appreciate you taking the time to answer these questions. I look forward to your response and working with you!

Phew!! "I need to have some other details" – *15 questions?* I guess this salesperson forgot it's all about what the prospect needs, not about what he, the salesperson, needs. I know what he is trying to do, but he is going about it all wrong, even if the prospect is a known quantity. He gave the prospect homework…a lot of homework! How about getting some of this information quickly over the phone and, based on the answers, determine whether setting up an appointment would even be appropriate? This note reeks of the attitude that the venue requires all sorts of information before it can decide to book you. By the time you get all those important details nailed down, your competition across the street will have picked up the phone, filled in all the missing blanks, established some rapport and set up an appointment (if warranted) for a site visit. The salesperson in this example needed 100% of the information now, before he could move to action. He was clearly not comfortable working within that "gray area" we talked about in the Introduction – the ability to let go and sense where the game is moving and then take action. In this case, all had to be spelled out in black and white in advance, because the salesperson was fearful and needed the security of knowing all the details. Details are always extremely important to the hesitant.

I purposely included this example, even though it is not a solicitation letter but a response to an inquiry. What you need to do in these situations is to change it up. You need to turn the inquiry around and convert it into a solicitation. You need to pick up the phone, not your mouse! By the end of this chapter, I think you will come away with some ideas as to how to change this from a reactive to a proactive situation.

A Word About...

...RFPs (requests for proposal). RFPs come from an assortment of channels and search engines, usually by email and usually marked "urgent" or "time sensitive." They are often blasted to multiple venues across various time zones and a selection of cities. Some salespeople consider these to be "leads." I admit I am not a big fan of RFPs. I think the danger is they can lead to knee- jerk reactive responses from both customers and salespeople. After all, an RFP removes human interaction from the sales process and can turn everything into a transaction. However; many companies today simply will not consider your venue unless you have submitted back to them a completed RFP. You need to learn how to respond quickly, effectively and efficiently so you will have the opportunity to compete in this segment. And I do believe you can do this without falling into the "it's all about dates, rates and space" game. And let's keep in mind –where do you expect to be in five or six years? I trust it's not constantly responding to RFPs.

A strategy many good salespeople employ to deal with an RFP (even when it states "do not contact by phone") is very similar to the email inquiry we just reviewed. They consciously make the decision to break through the email storm and call direct. Time is money, and that goes for an RFP, as well. You must always say to yourself, "What about my investment of time?" The best use their time management and pre-qualifying skills to quickly ascertain whether this is a legitimate lead.

I have never seen an RFP that did not raise other questions that need to be clarified and would thus require at least some minimal discussion. Most people will not take offense to your call; some would even welcome it. And, by the way, who made up the rule you can't contact someone by phone? For the sake of your own business and career, it might be good to start ignoring all those "do not call" notations. You can always say, "Oh I'm sorry...I did not notice that," then segue right into your own pre-qualification questions. It goes to that idea of living in the "So what?" zone not the "What if?" zone.

HERE'S HOW TO DO IT

STEP ONE: THE LETTER

If you want to differentiate yourself, send a letter. Given today's electronic communication barrage, receiving a letter is a unique experience. Plus, people like to see their names in writing; it makes them feel important and valued. A letter will get you the most attention and highest probability of an acceptance of your follow-up call. Your letter should be short – three—four paragraphs to one page in length. And talk like a real person, not a marketeer. Remember, this is the prospect's first exposure to you; it starts the formidable task you have of building trust. It can be as simple as this:

Dear _____,

I understand you are in charge of planning _____. I think you will be interested in us because this is exactly what we specialize in. With that thought in mind, I'll be calling you to set up an appointment (or: I look forward to speaking with you further in this regard in the near future). Until then I remain...

Sincerely Yours,

A more detailed and preferred example:

Dear _____,

I am writing to you because I understand you are directly involved with planning the Annual Dinner for (name of organization) each year.

I am pleased to let you know we have recently completed a total renovation/redesign of our Grand Ballroom. We have been privileged to be the site of some of the most prestigious and exciting fundraising events New York City has to offer, such as XX and XY and XZ. We would very much welcome the opportunity to be of service to your fine organization, as well.

Mr/Ms _____, thank you for the consideration you have already given my letter. I look forward to speaking with you further (or: I will be calling you shortly to further discuss) as to how the (your venue) might best serve the needs of (name of organization) in 2015. Until then I remain...

Optional: As noted, in a few instances, it can help to specify a few names of similar organizations you have worked with. You may also want to include one or two (maximum) photos of your venue, however I would avoid sending any brochures. I will explain why in a moment.

Note: You can easily substitute the word "corporation" or "association" or "school," etc., when referring to the organization. When referencing other organizations, you have worked with, make sure they are within the same market segment. Also, if you recently read an article about the organization (in a newspaper or journal) you should reference it and use that as a lead-in to your note.

STEP 2: THE CALL

This is where the rubber meets the road, where theory and reality collide – the follow-up call. This is your second contact with this prospective customer, so you really are not making a cold call at this point. Remember, it is not a solicitation call until you actually speak with the prospect. "I left a message" is not good enough. What happens on the call? Very simply:

> *Hi, this is (your name), from the XXX venue. I wrote to you the other day and indicated/promised that I would be calling you to discuss your future planning for the annual dinner.*

What just happened?

1. You connected directly with a potential customer.
2. You fulfilled your first promise: You made a small promise in that introduction letter and you kept it.
3. You won some points: You demonstrated that when you say something will happen, it does.
4. You have started to establish some credibility and presence.
5. You have subtly started to dictate play. You are executing *your* game plan. You are authoring *your* shots.

All of this results from a simple letter and a simple follow-up phone call. When you sent the letter, you got their attention for a very brief moment. If you follow up quickly, within a few days, they'll remember it. They are starting to formulate their first impression of you, whether that be on a conscious or an unconscious level. First impressions are *extremely important* in sales, because they are so hard to change. So, it is vitally important to start the process correctly.

This potential customer is starting to say things to themselves, such as, "This person has an interesting style, a nice/short note, to the point. He's on the phone now following up. That's professional." If nothing else you are communicating the message that you are straightforward, direct and transparent.

Note: Being professional and having good manners always go a long way toward establishing good relationships. Good relationships, in turn, create very successful careers.

Step 3: Two-Minute Warning

Now the clock is ticking. Literally. Once that person has picked up the phone, you have about two minutes; I call it "The Two-Minute Warning." Overwhelmingly, when a prospect takes your initial call, he is just being courteous. You went to the trouble of sending him a very nice, professionally written, respectful note, and respect is pretty high up on the list for most people. So, in most cases he is going to do the right thing and take your call.

Within two minutes, however, he will say to himself, "Why am I on this call? What's in it for me?" So, you need to move quickly, while the welcome mat is still out. In other words, you need to take the most aggressive step possible, as professionally as possible. You made a statement, and you are waiting a moment or two for his response. Make sure you do wait. Do not speak after you make your opening comment about discussing the event. If there is hesitation, or you get a vague, iffy kind of answer, challenge it, in a low-key way. For example:

> *I know you have been hosting your annual dinner for many years at _____. Would you be open to considering or exploring alternate venues for this event next year?*

Again, shut up and wait for a response. Notice, too, the words I used in the above statement—open to, consider, explore, alternate—these are softer, warmer, more inviting words. These words are not putting the person on the defensive. These words are inviting the person to have a conversation/ discussion with you. Any response other than "No, we are happy where we are," invites you to say, "Would you like to set up a meeting with me to discuss this further?" If the person hesitates again, press the issue a bit by saying:

*Look, I know your time is important and I very much ap-
preciate your taking my call. If you are happy where you are,
I will simply make a note of it and contact you next year.*

If the answer is "We are happy where we are," respond:

*I understand, and I can certainly appreciate your loyalty
to an establishment that has done an outstanding job for
you, as I would appreciate your loyalty if the situation were
reversed.*

You have concluded this part of your solicitation, but you have not
concluded soliciting altogether. Next question:

*May I ask you one other question (wait for them to respond)?
Are there any other people in your company (organization)
you know of who might be in need of my services?*

Based on your professional, straight-forward and pleasant approach
from the start, most people are inclined to try to help, if they can, if for
no other reason than it makes them feel good about themselves. Plus,
you did what they did not expect. You didn't continue pushing to sell
your venue to them. They're thinking you seem like a pretty confident
and respectful guy.

Remember, the goal of the call is only to get an appointment. To use
another bit of sports terminology, your "swing thought" is to advance
the call; advance it to the point of what action the potential customer
will agree to take next. The best times to make these calls? I would say
generally early in the morning when people are fresh. Decision-makers
tend to get in early; they have not been inundated yet with the huge assortment of problems, emails, meetings and frustrations we all encounter every day. Outside business hours can also be a good time to call;
you are less apt to get voicemail and these early birds are more apt to
cut to the chase and give you direct, honest answers to your questions.

Remember too, especially on the first follow-up call, you must be comfortable enough to let the prospect control the conversation. This is your opportunity to learn where their interests lie. Many salespeople are not comfortable with this "letting go" of control, and yet you must. Similar to tennis, a light grip on the racquet is what you are looking for.

Step 4: Initial Probing

While a prospect is considering your venue, some forget that you, too, must consider whether this prospect is worth your continued investment of time. In the initial stages of a tennis match, for example, a good tennis player takes the time to feel out the player and get a sense of how he plays. He'll hit an assortment of different shots – to the backhand, cross-court and a few short. In sales, depending on how long the prospect wants to stay on the phone, this sort of "feeling out" might gain you additional information. If the individual is talkative, you may even be able to ask a few more questions. If you listen carefully, you might pick up clues that have possible sales implications. This probing helps you avoid all those dead ends of solicitation that are usually based on the salesperson's assumptions. When you question in this manner, you are clarifying. Outlined below are a few suggested queries:

- How did it go this year?
- How many years have you been at this facility?
- Why are you looking?
- Have you ever been in our venue for an event before?
- Have you ever looked at us before? No? Oh, why's that?
- Did you look at us last year? No? Why not?

It's highly unlikely you are going to be able to ask, let alone secure, answers to most of these questions; with luck, you'll maybe get to one or two. However, these questions and your observations as to the tone of the responses and mental framework of the prospect are extremely important considerations. For many, this is often overlooked, in terms of potential ROI. The prospect's responses are all part of that immediate first impression – your gut reaction to them and them to you. Inexperienced and average salespeople just don't get this because every lead, every call, is a strong opportunity in their eyes, until suddenly it isn't. They are just talking and pressing, not listening and watching.

THE POWER OF WHY

"Why?" or "Why's that?" are great non-threatening questions. You will be amazed how much critical information you can pick up over the phone just by asking a few questions and then listening intently to the answers. Nobody really wants to just come out and tell you "No." If you can get the prospect to say, "No, I'm not open to looking at your facility for my event next year," then, with an eye to the future, you can say, "I see. Why is that?" And remember, say it with a smile; it does translate over the phone. This question just might lead to opening the door to a sale or at least make it clear why this organization will not use your facility. Either way, you've learned something valuable.

FIRST-TIME EVENTS

With new, first-time prospects, there is a slightly higher probability a prospect will be open to your venue for a number of reasons:

- They may have already outgrown the facility they contracted for the inaugural event.
- They may have encountered service issues, which are now turning them into Lookers and/or Shoppers.
- A few board members or senior executives might be pressing to change venues for the following year because that's what board members always seem to do.

It is the nature of new or first-time events for things to be unsettled. Now, of course, the venue that hosts a first-time event also has an extra plus in their favor. If it goes very smoothly, then the venue has bought itself a huge amount of goodwill and loyalty.

The same kind of dynamic can be in play with new leadership. Although with new leadership your odds are even better. In most cases, new leaders want to put their stamp on things. They want to demonstrate there's a new sheriff in town and things are not going to be done the same old way. New leadership wants to shake it up. Smart salespeople play off that need.

STEP 5: INITIAL QUALIFYING

What else is happening on your phone call? You're starting to qualify them. Granted, this is a preliminary qualification. You'll do an in-depth qualification if and when you land a site appointment. In this initial call, your goal is to try to sense the most likely answer to these questions that we first discussed in Chapter 2:

1. Does this person buy, need or want <u>exactly</u> what I am selling?
2. Is this person showing some <u>real</u> interest in possibly buying from me?
3. Can this person afford to host the event with us? Does he/she have the money?

This is where many salespeople go seriously off track, because they are afraid to ask themselves these questions – afraid the answer might be "No."

Throughout the solicitation process, you will always want to get to "No" quickly, so you can move on to those who can say "Yes." Think back to the example of the tasting I outlined in Chapter 4. If the sales manager had asked a few more questions early on, he would have known exactly where he was on that first phone call and the answer would have been – nowhere.

As a salesperson, you will make lots of calls and secure only a few appointments. That's just the nature of prospecting/solicitation. So, let's look at some of the inevitable stumbling blocks, the speed bumps, as I call them, that you will encounter at this stage in the game.

Step 6: Handling Those Inevitable (and Predictable) Objections on the First Call

Prospect Says: "I don't need your services now."

Your response: "So this might actually be the best time for us to talk. Once I get a better sense of your needs, maybe I will be able to suggest a better way of doing things for your future events. And then maybe when you do get to that point and need the services of a catering venue you will be more inclined to think of me and our facilities. What do you think?"

Prospect says: I haven't had any complaints and I have been using XXX for over four years now."

Your Response: "That's really very good for you; they are very fortunate to have your business. However, have you given any consideration to the possibility you could have an even better experience with us?"

Prospect Says: "I'm very busy right now."

Your Response: "When would be good for you?" The customer says, "Call me in three weeks." You say, "Of course, I certainly can do that," and then you follow up in three weeks and remind them in a nice way in your opening statement that, as requested, you are following up in three weeks. What if the response is "Call me in four months"? Response: "Ok, I can certainly do that, but let me ask you one other question. It has been my experience over the years that when someone says call me in four months, there are, more than likely, only two reasons for that response: One, you really do want to meet with me and I am very pleased you do or, two, you really don't want to meet with me and are figuring I will forget to follow up and essentially just go away. So, I guess my real question, with all due respect, is: Which dynamic do we have here? And please be candid, I will not be offended." Then shut up and listen for the answer. If there's an uncomfortable silence, even better. Remember, earlier we talked about the importance of time management and uncomfortable questions. This is a good example of that in action. You need to ask that question because that means you'll get to the root of the situation. And the root of it might be he is not really interested in you, and that's fine; you can then move on.

Prospect Says: "Send me some literature."

Your Response: "Sure; I can do that, but all that's going to do is tell you a lot about square footage, ceiling heights and ballroom dimensions. I think it is much more important to learn about your needs and goals for your events." Remember, you are trying to position having a meeting as a benefit to him. You are still qualifying. You are still looking for an open mind and you still need to ask some uncomfortable questions, in order to make best use of your time.

Prospect says: "I tried your venue once before and the service was very slow."

Your Response: "I'm very sorry to hear that. However, I would personally be handling your event from beginning to end, and I can assure you that is not the way I operate. What you just told me, I can tell you will not happen again. I would ask that you allow me the opportunity to show you exactly how we would make sure you do not encounter slow service ever again at our venue."

Prospect Says: "I'm happy with XXX Venue, but send me your price quotes."

This is a pretty insulting statement, but surprisingly many salespeople do just that. However, as a skilled salesperson, using good time management skills and exercising your right to ask challenging questions, you can better address the statement as follows:

Your Response: "I will do that, but first I want to sit down with you and learn more about exactly what you do and what you want and need." If this results in the all-important meeting, you will then have the opportunity to find out how pleased they really are or are not. You will want to address the quality, the service, the pricing, as well as the ease of doing business with their current facility. This might, or it might not lead to your being able to move further along in the selling process. After your meeting, you could say to this customer, "You have a pretty good arrangement where you are, but you could have even better. We could improve upon your current situation, which is why you should really give us further consideration." Many potential customers think "what I have right now is fine." You are asking them to consider that, yes, they do have a good arrangement now, but they could have a much better one in the future. You need to get them to thinking "better and future."

Remember, it's a waste of your important time to compete for a sale that does not exist. The price-quote/referencing scenario is a loser's game that you want to avoid at all costs. If the prospect refuses to meet, if nothing else, you have saved yourself a lot of time. He really had no interest. He had a closed mind.

By the way, the word "future" helps you in drawing the prospect away from defending his current venue and opens the conversation to be more of an exploratory one. It's a little less confrontational. The same applies when you first ask if the prospect would be open to exploring "alternative venues" for next year's event. It's a little thing, but important.

Voicemail. Now, what do you do if you get voicemail on your initial follow-up call? Since the objective is to get them to call you back, you need to sound important, successful, professional, positive and expectant. Leave the same opening message you opened with when an actual person answered the phone:

> *Hi, this is XXX from the XXX venue. I wrote to you the other day. I indicated (I promised) I would be calling to discuss your annual dinner. If you could please call me back at your earliest convenience that would be great.*

Second Voicemail. If you do not receive a call back in two or three days, then you need to call back. If you get voicemail again, at this point, you need to tell him why he should call you back; you need to up the ante, so to speak, with a more personalized message. Is it your experience? Is it your hard work? Or is it your enthusiasm? You need to give him a compelling reason to respond to you. For example:

> *Hi Mr.---, this is XXX from the XXX venue. I'm sure you are inundated with calls every day from all sorts of people. I think you should return my call though, and here's why. I have been with the XXX venue for X years and I think my knowledge and experience in fundraising events could be of value to you. I also know that if you were to talk to my customers — some of whom I'm sure you already know — they would tell you exactly the value I have brought to their business and events for over 20 years. If that would be of interest to you, I would urge you to call me. Thank you and I look forward to speaking with you soon.*

Now, why would I leave a message like that? Well, in the real world of sales most people change venues because they feel their business is being taken for granted. They might say it is due to service issues, but the root cause of the service issue is that the venue took them for granted. So, if a prospective customer got a voicemail message like that from a competing facility, the odds are pretty good he or she would return that call. Here's another approach:

> *I'm fairly new at (venue). However; I don't think you are going to find anyone who is going to have a better under- standing and focus on the need to work hard to earn and keep your business. If that is an important criterion for you, then I urge you to please call me back at…."*

What do I hear? I hear a hungry, enthusiastic salesperson on the phone looking to make his or her mark. Enthusiasm can be just as compelling a reason as experience for someone to respond. It goes back to what we talked about earlier: Most people respond positively to someone who is authentic and genuine.

Always ask them to call you back. You deserve it, you're entitled to it, you expect it and you should act like you expect it. It all goes back to your mindset: Are you playing to win or are you afraid to lose? Or, to put it another way: "Your attitude, not your aptitude, will determine your altitude," as Zig Ziglar always used to say.[43]

Great salespeople expect to win. They first sell the customer on themselves, then on their company. And you are definitely selling yourself on this second call.

Occasionally, when I was unsuccessful reaching someone (many people screen their calls) I used my personal cell phone. This usually works, and the added element of surprise usually pays off with some quick, direct questions and answers.

Still No Response? Now it's time to reach out to an assistant or someone who works closely with the prospect. It could be you'll find out the person you wrote to has been dealing with a personal issue that has precluded them from responding.

And Still No Response? Well, now the only option is to send an email – the least preferred method of communication. This is what I would say in such an email:

> *I have tried contacting you several times. I wrote to you recently and have followed up by telephone to see if you have any need of our services and my expertise. I certainly thought you would, based upon what I currently know about your organization and events. I just wanted to reach out one last time to see if there is any interest at all on your part. Thank you and I would appreciate your response."*

---

[43] Ziglar.com

Admittedly, you are pushing the envelope a little bit here, but at this point, you've got nothing to lose. So, go for it! You will feel better if you do. You will know you have given it your all.

If you still get no response, it's time to accept there is no interest, at least not right now. "No" doesn't mean never, it just means not yet. Don't take it personally; rejection is part of the game. Learn from it. The situation could and usually does change. One positive outcome is that you will have cut your losses; you've been honest enough with yourself to realize this isn't going anywhere, so let's move on. This saves time. You can retreat now, so you can live to fight another day.

WHO IS THE COMPETITION?

You might think you are competing against a specific venue, but this is a very narrow view. In fact, you are always competing against the prospective customer's current situation, their status quo. What do I mean by that? It is a physical, mental and emotional state. All three have to be addressed. Are they really open to looking at you and your venue or not? Your challenge as a salesperson is to break through the customer's natural tendency to stay put. If they are happy/settled where they are, you need to try to get them to be open to moving. And if they are moving – in other words, if they're actively looking around at different venues – you need to turn them in your direction. I gave the example earlier of the fundraising organization looking to move their dinner to another venue, until they found out a major renovation project was going to take place. They were moving and were just about to sign with the other facility, but we turned them back in our direction.

WHAT AM I LOOKING FOR?

Throughout the entire solicitation process, always look for a good attitude and, just as important, an open mind from the prospect. For example: "Yes, I'd be happy to talk with you," or "I see the value in what you're saying." Look out for bad attitudes, as well, for example: "Things are working just fine where we are currently hosting the event. I don't see any need to fix anything." "Call me in four months," or "I'm not willing to pay your prices." These responses indicate a closed mind; they are staying put, no need to waste your time trying to convince them to move. But give up entirely? No! Put them back on trace for further follow-up. That person may leave the organization in two years and someone with a more open attitude may take his place.

WHAT ARE THEY LOOKING FOR?

Lastly, you are competing against that inborn human attitude: "What's in It for Me?" I have heard this referred to as "everyone's favorite radio station."

- What's in it for my organization?
- What's in it for me personally?
- Are you going to make my life easier?
- Are you going to make my life harder?

Granted, on this first call you cannot gain the full picture, but you can get some sense of it. Identify and respond to these unspoken questions for each particular prospect as you move through the sales process. If you cannot demonstrate to a potential customer what's in it for them – their potential ROI – you've lost them. Very early on in the sales process the best salespeople identify what benefits (tangible and intangible) are most important to each prospective customer.

You need to always be thinking about what benefit could be the most important to this particular buyer. This is the "strike zone," the "sweet spot" – the element that is central to the buyer. You must start searching for it on that very first call.

THE END GAME

Build a pipeline, with lots of real prospects, not maybes. Fill it with leads for this quarter, next quarter, next year, and even two years from now. Building your pipeline builds confidence, which in turn reduces fear and anxiety and makes you a better salesperson. You suddenly find you have options. You realize you can walk away from all those Price Hounds and tenuous leads. In a nutshell:

> The Larger Your Prospect Pipeline:
>
> The less time you will have to...
> The less time you will need to....
> The less time you will want to...
> ... spend on people with a bad attitude *(e.g. Price Hounds)*.

TAKEAWAYS:

Ineffective salespeople don't have conversations, they have emails.

Email is the enemy of solicitation; the telephone is your friend.

Professional solicitation leads to more value-based (not price-based) conversations.

As in tennis, good solicitors take the ball early. Bad solicitors procrastinate — wait for the ball to come to them and end up getting run around the court.

Great salespeople (like good hunters) are always hungry and make sure they always have something to eat.

Solicitation is a lot like writing. If you want to be a good writer, you must write every day. You can always edit/revise a poor page, but you can never edit a blank page.

Smile while on the telephone — yes, it comes through, it shows confidence and indicates that you are not out to force anything on anybody.

A smile greatly encourages the prospective customer to be more candid and direct with you, as well.

Solicitations that are going nowhere ("the illusion of selling") tend to be very drawn-out and prolonged. This is a clear sign to cut your losses and move on, which some just don't see.

With Solicitation: Get in and get out quickly.

"Networking makes them feel uncomfortable and phony. Many understandably see networking on the surface as... exploitative and inauthentic." [44]

[44] "Learn to Love Networking," Harvard Business Review, May 2016, Tiziana Casciaro, Francesca Gino and Maryam Kouchaki.

CHAPTER 6

Networking

I will admit, on the surface, the above sentiments are quite prevalent and, regrettably, often true when networking is conducted inauthentically. There is good reason, though, why networking – both formal and informal – has been around for over 2,000 years. We touched on it in Chapters 1 and 2. Be authentic, non-exploitative and don't suck up to people – it's really that simple. And let's not overlook the two most important truisms of a good networker:

- A simple, friendly, sociable attitude is key.
- Authenticity + Lack of Vanity/Pride = Likeability.

Anyone who has advanced in his or her career has had to learn the art of networking. When done correctly, networking can be a very effective, forward-thinking way to grow contacts for both personal and professional purposes. As pointed out earlier in this book, entrepreneurs, small business owners and immigrants have a huge advantage over others – particularly those in a corporate environment – when it comes to networking. For their very survival, they must work hard to understand what is going on in a customer's mind and in their world. They do this by actively interacting with a diverse range of individuals on a regular basis and listening carefully.

Networking is essentially all about meeting and engaging people, establishing some kind of rapport and finding common ground. As you get to know people, you expose yourself to opinions, viewpoints and potential business opportunities you never even imagined. All sorts of opportunities "reveal" themselves. And, when executed correctly and consistently, you can positively influence others.

Networking is a combination of two seemingly contradictory strengths: planning and discipline, plus the ability to be spontaneous – knowing how to mingle with people. When your networking has a structure and a purpose, it naturally leads to action, and positive actions most often lead to positive results. And, of course, networking helps you become much less reliant on all those random telephone and email inquiries that seem to seldom materialize.

NETWORKING BASICS

All great networkers incorporate most of the following concepts into their day-to-day activities:

Start Now	Stay in Touch
Go Wide	Keep It Moving
Have and Practice a Routine	Dress Appropriately
Take it Easy	Keep It Positive/Current
Give and Take	Arrive Happy
Listen	Read and Respond to Body Language
Do Online Research	

Let's take a look at each of these basics:

Start Now: Networking is generally a long-term proposition. It doesn't just happen because you decided to go network today. It takes time, practice and patience before you see some results, so don't put it off.

Go Wide: People tend to limit their networking to business associates and people they already know and like. But that's just the start. Almost anyone you know or meet could be in a position to help you, and you them. Your immediate close business contacts are probably where you'll have your best chances of initial success, so start by going to events where your customers and potential customers are most likely to be. After that, you need to push yourself to expand that circle. Openness is a big key to any coordinated networking plan. Most of us surround ourselves with people who are just like ourselves; however, it always pays to expand your network to include people who are not like you – those from very different ethnic groups, professions, educational backgrounds, ages and incomes. In the case of networking, less is not more.

Almost every situation presents networking opportunities Waiting for a bus, going to a sporting event, walking your dog, even waiting in line in a store can be the start of a networking relationship. Strike up a conversation with someone nearby, then segue into what that person does for a living. You never know what unexpected results might materialize.

Have and Practice a Routine: Networking is just like any sport or exercise; you need to perform the same routine over and over and over to build "muscle memory"– just like any athlete. Sheer repetition will improve your results. If you go to an event and you don't connect with anyone, analyze your performance. Ask yourself: "What did I do wrong?"

Extend your hand first. Make it your practice to be the first to reach out your hand, say hello and initiate the conversation, rather than wait to be approached. As in tennis, your serve and accompanying footwork launch you into the game by pulling your body into the court. In the case of networking, you'll want to launch yourself into a conversation and get into the game. You are then on offense – a nice place to be when you get comfortable with it.

Take it Easy: A big mistake some networkers make is coming on too strong, making people pull away. Think of your first contact with someone as the start of a process. If you go into this conversation thinking you'll get to that one person and sell them something, you are way off base. It just doesn't work that way.

Give and Take: When attempting to network, too many people focus on taking, when you really need to focus on giving. The best way to get something will always be to give something, but many overlook this. Take a genuine interest in the other person before you ask him to take an interest in you. If you focus in this direction, you will start to see all sorts of opportunities to be helpful.

Listen: Listening is one of our "Pillars" and also one of the most underrated skills in networking. Listen for remarks that imply assistance, such as, "I don't know," "I need," "I want," or "I can't" – all of these statements are essentially saying "I need help," and if you can, then do so and help wherever possible. Keep your focus on the other person – not on you – and your listening skills will automatically improve. The real sales greats listen twice as much as they talk. However, when they do talk their comments are always directed back to the person they are speaking with in the form of a question. Most of the also-rans do just the opposite.

SOME COCKTAIL PARTY CONVERSATION STARTERS

- How do you know the host (or host organization)?
- What's your connection to this event?
- Do you know anything about the speaker?
- How did you get involved in working for *(name of their company)* …or working in the *(name of industry)*?

These kinds of open-ended questions get the ball rolling and draw people out, versus questions that only require a "Yes" or "No" answer. You'll also want your body and facial language to communicate openness and a welcoming attitude. In your follow-up questions, dig a little deeper, building on their initial responses. In so doing, you will further convey your authenticity and that you have been actively participating in the conversation. The skilled salesperson knows all people on a very fundamental level want to know you really hear them, that you really see them. By looking at the person (not looking around the room to see if there is someone else more prominent you should be talking to) you show you are engaged. Similarly, making good eye contact, and sitting or standing straight further round out the picture. You will exude a positive energy, appear relaxed, calm and in the moment. You'll look like someone others would like to talk with. Isn't this right in line with what we discussed in Chapter 2: Active-Focused Listening?

Research Online: Face-to-face communication is always best, but online networking does have something to offer. LinkedIn, for example, is an excellent professional networking resource. Take advantage of it when you can. Neiman Marcus's 4,500 associates communicate with customers via their company-issued iPhones on their Instagram and Snapchat accounts, using an app called iSell. The company encourages customers to follow sales associates on social media because, "Customers who are attached to a sales associate spend more." This is per Karen Katz, CEO, who spoke at the National Retail Federation meeting. *New York Post,* January 21,2018.

"The Flip Side." While you must engage with such sites as LinkedIn, Facebook and Twitter, don't overplay the role of social media in the sales process. We have all met people who are very facile with these websites, and yet in person are totally devoid of social skills. Embrace social media – use it to your advantage – but keep in mind the best way to get someone's attention is still decidedly old school – stick your hand out and introduce yourself.

Stay in Touch: Believe it or not, many people never follow up. Big mistake. Within a week (better yet, within 24 hours) of meeting someone who is or could be a good networking contact, send him or her a quick email or a short note telling them how nice it was to meet them and how much you appreciate the time they spent with you. Next, stay in touch. For a smaller select group, do so every three or four months, maybe by giving that person a quick call or sending an email or an invite to a local event that might be of interest. But keep it casual; you don't want to annoy people by constantly sending emails. Friendly contact is what we're seeking here.

Keep It Moving: If you find yourself spending more than five minutes with someone and the conversation is going nowhere, then you're basically wasting your time. If someone is just talking at me, then I know I have to get away. If he is so into himself, he is not going to be a good networking contact. If you need to end the discussion at an event, here are a few friendly techniques that work well:

- Ask to exchange business cards; this tends to help in putting an end to a fruitless networking conversation.

- If that doesn't work, remind the person that networking events are about meeting as many people as possible and suggest the two of you continue to do just that.

- Another option would be to politely introduce yourself and the individual to a new person or group. Then, once the conversation starts to flow, you can excuse yourself.

Dress Appropriately: Always dress appropriately for the occasion. Is it business attire or business casual? When in doubt, err on the side of dressing more conservatively. The way you are dressed will add or subtract from your power to influence and for both of you to listen.

Keep it Positive/Current: Talk about subjects and other people in a positive manner. Stay up to date through newspapers, financial publications, television news; you will always be able to glean a few highlights to employ when you initiate a conversation.

Arrive Happy: No matter what kind of day you are having, put it all out of your mind. People are more attracted to another person's warmth as conveyed by good eye contact and a nice smile.

Read Non-Verbal Cues: Don't overlook non-verbal communication – both yours and theirs. Notice the subtle cues, including body language:

- People who are open to new relationships have an open stance; hands are at their sides. And their stance is turned outward.

- Three or four people in a circle standing face to face and engaged in an intense conversation are usually too busy at that moment to welcome a new person.

- People who mirror the speaker's gestures, tilt their head at the same angle or at the same time shift their weight onto one foot, signal a desire to show they are on the same page with the speaker and are into the conversation.

- People who are open often lead conversations but all the other people in the group are also engaged. All tend to nod frequently, have strong mutual eye contact and lean forward.

- People are not attracted to a person who is name dropping or talking on and on about his or her resume, competence or connections. Just the opposite. Good networkers show much more interest in what the other person has to say.

- Leaning back? This body language is saying you don't particularly like the person you are speaking with.

- Avoid using words such as "great," "awesome" and "fantastic." They are overused, ineffective and, worse, sound inauthentic.

- Domineering people tend to talk most of the time and avoid eye contact with both their listeners and anyone else in the vicinity.

Always Be Networking

You don't have to be overbearing about it and, I know, it sounds a little bit like that old sales expression "Always be closing," but you do need to make networking a part of your daily activities. You will not find customers at every event, but every event is an opportunity to meet people, build a network of individuals who can help, who can make referrals or who may eventually become customers – even friends.

THE NETWORKER'S DAILY DRILL

What are some of the more tactical steps we can take on an everyday basis? My advice on how to network is pretty simple:

A. Become A Joiner: It goes back to that key habit of "Connecting" we talked about. Join one or two organizations and be active in those organizations. By being an active member, I don't just mean attending member events, though that's very important. I mean volunteer to be on one of the committees or even take on a Board position with the organization. It takes a certain commitment, in terms of time and energy, but it usually reaps huge rewards. The best way to maximize your return on membership dues is by being an active member. I am a member of NACE (National Association of Catering and Events). In fact, I am one of the two founding members of the NACE New York chapter. At various times over the years, I served on the Board as Programs and Membership Chair, as well as President of the chapter.

Another approach: If you are a member of your local chamber of commerce, try to take on a leadership role and/or make yourself available to speak at a chamber event every few months. If you speak for 20 minutes on a topic, you will meet about 40-50 new people. Do the same with a similar organization every other month, such organizations as the Business Networking Institute, a trade industry association, or even the Lions Club or Rotary (if you think there is realistically some business potential there). Do this for six months and you will have met about 300 new contacts. The same principle applies to doing volunteer work for a charity in your community. You will meet like-minded people who share many of the same goals. Why not join your college alumni association, or see if they have an alumni mentoring program? I joined mine, and that resulted in securing a $40,000 piece of business.

By the way, in most cases, I suggest going alone to these types of events. This forces you to make contact with other people. You will have a lot more power and control than you might expect. You can decide when to enter or leave a conversation, or even when to leave the event entirely. It also prevents you from socializing with friends or co-workers versus networking with people you do not know. Sometimes, salespeople attend events and are very comfortable just talking with each other or, at most, talking with a customer they have done business with for over 20 years. Conversely, the idea here is to meet new people and to be slightly uncomfortable.

B. Arrive Early: Easy enough to do. You can help set up and you will have the opportunity to greet people, as well. What a way to network! This can also lead to being introduced to key people.

C. Have Your Introduction Ready: Have a quick, short, interesting answer to the question "What do you do or who are you with?" Remember it's not a sales pitch. It is a few short sentences that point toward the potential value you offer (your "value proposition"). It should be something that will get them focused on wanting to know more about you. You only get one chance to make your first impression; it's always best to keep it short and snappy. When creating your value proposition, consider the value you offer people, both personally and professionally. Try to answer some of the most logical initial questions a person might have about you and your company, such as:

- What do your clients enjoy because of your company's work?
- What attributes does your company possess that people value?
- What is your personal brand promise?
- What is your company's brand promise?
- When does your company come up as a problem solver?

With this as your reference point, reflect this information back in your introduction.

Using "you" in your introduction gets you immediate attention and involves your audience on a much more personal basis. For example, if you were a financial advisor you might say, "I help people like you plan for their long-term financial dreams. I manage most of the downside risk and help maximize the upside as much as possible." A person in real estate might say, "I help people like you make what, for most, is the biggest financial and buying decision of their lives." A person specializing in weddings might say: "I help people like you plan what many consider to be the most important day in their lives." Keep it all about them. A short 15- to 20-word phrase achieves maximum impact. Whatever it is, make sure your introduction is crystal clear in your own mind. If you totally believe it in a deep, personal way, other people will, too.

D. Be Specific and Direct: Good networkers focus on getting good input. When you ask contacts for information, don't be too general, ask for specific information. This helps avoid any confusion. Start by asking for their advice or their opinion. Since most people want to be helpful, this can help build the rapport you need to establish before asking for something else.

E. Nurture Your Contacts: When you've made a particularly valuable new contact, it's a very good idea to send the individual a personalized, handwritten thank-you note. It stands out as a way to let that person know you appreciate their help and value their input. This applies even more so if you book a piece of business through a networking contact. Let them know just how much you appreciate their help and value their input. How about sending a new contact a quick follow-up note suggesting you meet for coffee? Then, when you meet, provide him with one or two leads from your network that might be useful to him.

F. Networking at Work: "Ask and Volunteer" – two key words in any career – to be on relevant task forces and projects, or take on new responsibilities that highlight your skills and link you to decision-makers within your own organization. Key relationships often develop from collaborative work on company taskforces and projects. Let others know – especially your boss – that you are open to these opportunities.

Note: Be very selective as to which projects you take on. You do not want to be on one of those committees I referenced earlier that take "minutes" but waste hours.

In the same vein, be known as the "Go-To" person within your company for a particular type of account, market or sales strategy. If you can establish that kind of reputation within your company and deliver on it, you will grow your network. The same applies with being a specialist, as we discussed earlier.

Networking at a Convention or Corporate Conference

If approached strategically, conventions offer a prime opportunity for career advancement. In this situation, the playing field is leveled; there is no one you should not or could not be speaking with. With a bit of discipline, you can mix fun with landing contacts, learn the latest industry developments and generate sales. Here are a couple of tips for working a convention:

1. **Be prepared.** Your convention experience will be much more efficient with a few minutes of preparation. Try to get a list of attendees in advance. Many organizers are willing to share this information to help drive attendance. Select the people you want to meet from this list and then schedule time with them. Of course, also do some prep work on the speakers you'd like to hear from and meet. When the time comes for you to make an impression after the presentation, you'll come across as knowledgeable.

2. **Wear Your Name Tag.** It makes you more approachable and helps encourage conversations. Wear it to all convention events.

3. **Choose Targets Wisely.** While it might be tempting to wait in line to say hello to the major keynote speaker, it pays bigger dividends to introduce yourself to the lesser known but still very interesting speakers who may be standing alone. The reality is the celebrity types aren't going to remember 74 of the 75 people who approach them, but the lesser known speakers are very apt to remember you.

4. **Leave Your Comfort Zone.** Don't stick to presentations covering familiar topics; you're there to learn. Step out of your comfort zone and learn something new.

5. **Use Good Manners.** Etiquette is simply showing respect and kindness to everyone around you. A dearth of manners can go a long way toward making a bad impression. There are numerous books and – even training courses – that cover the subject in depth, from business to social etiquette – the full spectrum. If your manners need sprucing up, make it happen.

6. **Take notes.** If you are doing it right, you're going to shake hands with hundreds of people at a convention; it's like a cyclone of information. Unfortunately, when you leave, you can end up not following up on any of it – because you forget. So, carry a notepad or use a smart phone and make notes, record your promises, or simply scrawl them on the back of business cards. Follow up on all those connections you promised to make, the articles you promised to send and the luncheons you promised to schedule.

7. **Be in the room.** Everybody notices when a presentation speaker is disengaged; they also notice when an audience member is texting away or working on a laptop. You are delivering messages all the time and people around you pick up on them.

- **Attend** all social events. Do not go back to your room to catch up on your work from the office.
- **Circulate.** Step out of your comfort zone. Avoid the temptation to stagnate or to sit with people you know.
- **Participate.** Speak up and engage people. This allows you and everyone around you the opportunity to make connections.

8. **Share the Wealth**. You can build up good will back at the office by sharing what you've learned at the convention with your team.

9. **Always Carry Your Business Card**, and make sure it is easily accessible. The best time to exchange is when you first meet. Make it a part of your graceful introduction so that there's no anxiety as to when you do the exchange. If you are not offered a card, which can happen, simply ask for one. People seem relieved when you do this, and if someone doesn't give you a business card, relax; don't make a big deal of it.

10. **Take Your Time.** Don't dash through the trade show just so you can say you were there. Instead, challenge yourself to learn three new things about your products or your industry.

11. **Eating and Networking Don't Mix.** Most of us have tried to juggle food and a beverage while also trying to exchange business cards. Networking and eating are mutually exclusive activities, except when you're sitting down, so do one or the other. I usually find I'm not eating very much while networking. As a matter of fact, I suggest you eat before attending the event. And here's a tip: Carry a drink in your left hand so your right hand is always free to extend in a welcoming handshake to someone new.

12. **Execute "The Save."** Let's say you're attending a convention with your boss or teammate. If he or she doesn't immediately introduce you to someone they have met, that's a cue your partner can't remember the person's name. So, step up, introduce yourself and get the person's name and then repeat it. You've just saved your teammate.

13. **Join Them.** If you walk into a breakout session and see someone sitting alone at a table, go join them. It's hard to believe, but a lot of people see someone sitting alone and then they go sit at another table by themselves. Go figure.

14. **"Free Night."** What are you going to do on your "free night"? Instead of you and your team going out for dinner together, how about dividing up your team and have them each put together a dinner group of new people or associates from other areas of the country. That would be a little bit more interesting and, perhaps, fruitful.

15. **"Step In."** One of the most dynamic ways to network is to ask a question in front of a group at a convention or a large conference. You'll have a wonderful opportunity to introduce yourself to everybody in the room. And guess what? After the conference, people will come up to you to talk further about your question. Ideally, you will want to sit near the front of the room. Try to be one of the first with your hand up with your question. People will tend to remember it and you more easily. Be sure to introduce yourself and your company, speak clearly, loudly and get to the point with a straightforward direct question. Do it all in about 30 seconds.

Step in at meals by:

"Being the Gracious Host." While sharing a meal, assume the role of host. If there are extra place settings, ask the waiter to remove them. It's hard to carry on a conversation when there is a large gap at the table. If there is a tall table number stand on your table, ask the waiter to remove it as well, thereby opening up the table and allowing for unimpeded conversation. Make it a point as well to get up, walk over and introduce yourself to each person who comes to sit at your table.

"Being All-Inclusive." Throughout the meal, remain cognizant of people who seem to be on the sidelines or left out of the conversation. Do as much as you can to draw them into the conversation. Sometimes just making eye contact with the individual is enough to spur them on to enter the conversation.

You can also employ your stepping-in skills right at home in your own venue by:

"Greeting the Head Table." Make it a point to greet all the guests at the head table on any of the association, business or charitable luncheon/dinners you currently work with. There are usually one or two people at the head table who are decision-makers for other events. And, of course, your client will usually be willing to put in a good word on your behalf.

"Conducting A Tasting." It's a great opportunity to get to know a person or persons on a much deeper more personal level, and in a relaxed and enjoyable environment. Be the first at the table to initiate questioning, but keep it to all non-business topics. You just never know where the conversation will lead.

TAKEAWAYS:

When you network correctly, you will find yourself open to others and will start seeing the world from their perspective.

The opportunities are everywhere, and they are endless.

Stepping in goes right to the concept of changing your actions to change your thinking.

To be a decent golfer, you have to play at least twice a week. The same applies with networking.

Go solo as much as possible to networking events; it forces you to interact with new people.

"Death of a Salesman"[45]

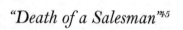

---

[45] From *Arthur Miller's Collected Plays*, 1957. Library of America.

CHAPTER 7

Electronic Communication

Email, tweets, texts and other forms of electronic communication have brought dramatic and profound change to the marketplace. Instant accessibility, efficiency, simplicity and speed to market are but a few of technology's major benefits. These are extremely powerful tools to help you connect and maintain contact with both existing and potential new customers. They do not, however, replace the human connection.

Emails and the like become problematic when they start to entirely replace face-to-face and telephone conversation. The more you remove yourself from direct face-to-face interactions, the clearer and more precise you need to be to avoid being misunderstood. And, even when you believe your words are clear, there is no guarantee that you are actually communicating with the recipient – you have no auditory or visual cues to confirm this. Like anything else, your success with email, etc., is dependent on how you use it, misuse it and/or abuse it.

OUT-OF-OFFICE MESSAGES

Many approach out-of-office emails and voicemails as last-minute, casual necessities, placed with little forethought .When set-up correctly, they present you with another important form of communication. As a salesperson, your goal is to create email/voicemail out-of-office messages that read and sound engaging, are professional and – most importantly – differentiate you from all the rest. Here are a few examples of actual out-of-office email messages that failed to meet this objective:

Out-of-Office Message 1:

Thank you for your email. I am currently out of the office with limited access to my email or voicemail. To ensure your questions are answered in a timely manner, you can expect a response within 24 hours from Mr. X. If you would like to speak with Mr. X directly, please call xxx-xxx-xxxx.

Thank you again for your interest in the X venue.

What I like about this message is that you are referred to a specific person. I think we all know most out-of-office messages do not do that. I also like that the person has indicated they will at least occasionally check for messages. It certainly is a more engaging message than most. The kicker is the customer has no idea who "Mr. X" is, nor his role in your operation. All the customer is thinking is: "Can this guy make it happen for me?" That's really what is of most importance to any customer or prospective customer.

(Slightly Negative) Out-of-Office Message 2:

Thank you for your email. I am currently out of the office without access to email August 23-27. If you need immediate assistance, please email my Administrative Assistant at xxxxx@xxxx. I look forward to following up with you at my earliest opportunity. Best regards.

In this case, notice the use of the word "My": *My* assistant (or in other instances, *My* event manager or *My* banquet captain). I cringe whenever I hear it. This word implies that either a lot of people work for you and/or you think using these terms makes you sound more professional and in charge. People do not work for you or me, and they are most definitely not "your" anything. Your assistant works "with" you or "for" you. You can decide which – I prefer "with"; it sounds more positive. Most important, I can't tell you how many times I have heard of customers calling to book an event, only to be directed to an assistant who should not be expected to pick-up where the sales manager left off. I'm not saying often but often enough, the customer gets frustrated and turns elsewhere. And as far as emailing the assistant, I think that is a little cold. Providing a telephone number as well would be a little bit more helpful and encouraging.

Notice too, the use of "my" a second time: "I look forward to following up with you at *my* earliest opportunity." This is even worse than the first. It seems to imply that when it's most convenient for you. In these instances, the salesperson usually finds out that when it is convenient for him to follow up, whatever opportunity that did exist is now long since gone.

(SLIGHTLY NEGATIVE) OUT OF OFFICE MESSAGE 3:

> *Thank you for your email. Please note I have a group in house and will be away from the office for most of the day, August 18-24. I will reply to your email upon my return. If you need immediate assistance, please contact my Assistant at xxx-xxx-xxxx. Thank you and have a great day!*

My first reaction: Based on how this message reads, it is not a stretch to think I might not hear back from you for six or even seven days – an eternity in the business world! My second reaction is if you were calling about your "group" that will be hosting a meeting in this venue in six weeks, I suspect you might think you are a pretty important person. However; you are apparently not as important as the immediate group that is here this week. Take heart though, because in five weeks you will be the most important group. And lastly *my* assistant – enough said on that one!

"Group," "off property," "group in house" – this is all catering jargon, cold and impersonal. By extension, the reader is led to believe this facility must be a very busy place with groups in and out all the time. You have effectively planted a seed in the customer's mind that you are too busy to talk with them. And you are the salesperson! Bottom line: Why go there? Why take the chance of leaving a customer with that perception?

Negative Out-of-Office Message 4:

Hello and thank you so much for your email. I will be out of the office on Thursday, May 2nd and Friday, May 3rd with limited access to emails. Your message is important to me, so I will do my best to reply as soon as I am able. If you need assistance setting up a site visit for Thursday, May 2nd or Friday, May 3^{rd,} please feel free to email Ms. X. She will do her best to assist you in setting up a site with someone on our team. For site visits for Monday, May 7th or future, I will respond to your email shortly. I will return to the office on Monday, May 7th with full access to email and voicemail. Thank you so much for your patience and have a great day.

Okay, there's a lot to critique here:

- The assistant "will do her best" to set up a site "with someone" on our team. Again, less than a stellar response. The customer doesn't want your assistant to try; they expect you to get it done.
- "Set up a site" – again, hotel jargon. How about speaking in simple English? For example, "setting up a site visit," or even better, "arranging an appointment"?
- "…with someone on our team"? You mean you are going to get just any old someone on the team to meet with me to discuss my important event?
- Finally, in this case, May 7 was a Tuesday not a Monday, so the final takeaway is you don't even know what day it is and yet – seriously – you want my business?

What Were They Thinking?

When these individuals sent these out-of-office notes, I don't think they realized what they were actually communicating. In fact, they would probably be shocked to be told these messages come across as disconnected, in some cases funny and, in others, slightly rude and condescending.

Although I think message #4 is clearly negative, messages #1-3 are lacking in the sense they are just not that engaging and, that all important word, "differentiating." They do not differentiate the salesperson from all the other emails everybody receives every single day.

What is the Customer Thinking?

When you turn it around and look at all these messages from a customer's or potential customer's vantage point, in one way or another, all of these emails are saying "Don't bother me, I'm not connected, I don't and will not have any idea what is going on until I return. You are essentially on your own. And as far as access? Today everybody has access (if they want to). So, really – wouldn't a better out-of-office email or voicemail be as follows?

Positive Out-of-Office Message:

> *Thank you for your email (or call). I will be out of the office beginning XX and returning on XX. In the interim I would like to suggest contacting (Full name), who works with me and is very familiar with all the events/organizations I work with. (Assistant first name) will be glad to assist you in any way possible in my absence. (Assistant first name) can be reached at (telephone #). You can also press zero and speak directly with (name) right now, if you prefer.*
>
> *(Assistant first name) and I will be in contact throughout my absence. I'm sure with (Assistant's first name) able assistance, we can take care of any questions you need addressed. Thank you and have a great day!*

That's demonstrating customer focus – a perfect example of being proactive, stepping up and stepping in. You just distinguished yourself from all the rest, as well. An existing customer or, even more importantly, a potential new customer, knows (even if it will be someone else getting back to them) they are okay with it because they know you are still involved. You coordinated it, you made it happen...for them. It demonstrates that even though you are not there, you are still on your game and don't take anything – especially the customer – for granted. As noted in Chapter 2, never underestimate the power of little things. So too, having a knowledgeable assistant who knows your customers, recognizes their voices on the telephone and can engage on many levels with those customers is a big plus for you as a salesperson.

"The Assumed Sale via Email Illusion":

Some salespeople actually try to accomplish much of their selling by email alone. Can you imagine?

> ***Salesperson:*** *Hi Karen. Would you be interested in using the Crystal Ballroom on June 12 for this event? It's the same space you are hosting your awards luncheon on September 28. By the way, are you ready to secure the space on September 28 with a contract for the luncheon?*

> ***Customer response:*** *Hi and thank you for getting back to me about the June 12 date. We decided to go in another direction for the September luncheon so we will not be moving forward with a contract.*

> ***Salesperson's loser response:*** *May I ask which venue you selected and if there is a particular reason? After keeping the space on hold for so long, we are disappointed to learn this today as we turned away other events. Any information you have regarding your sudden change is appreciated.*

> ***Better yet customer response:*** *I understand the VP in charge of the event has a long relationship with the other venue. He spent a long time discussing the event with the other venue and so, while it may seem to be a sudden change, they had been in conversation for quite some time and evaluated all the options.*

Game, Set, Match!

I guess the salesperson in question here didn't pick up on all the non-verbal communication or, should I say, the lack of communication over the last few weeks. But what a difference a simple phone call or two along the way and asking a few direct questions could have made. Notice as well, the "VP" actually spent time "talking with someone" at the other venue. The salesperson also made the terrible mistake of commenting about turning away other events. This attempt at making the customer feel guilty never works. Plus, if you really were in that situation, wouldn't you have called to reconfirm and make them aware of a potential challenge for the date? The only thing accomplished here is the potential customer feels disrespected by and distrustful of the salesperson. It's highly doubtful they will be calling again.

Takeaways:

Electronic correspondence is primarily to document, not to communicate.

With email, refusing to commit has never been easier.

There is more to be gained talking than emailing or texting, and there is potentially more to lose by emailing versus talking.

Ask yourself: "Is this email necessary? Would a telephone call or personal visit be more appropriate and effective for the situation?"

Speak directly as soon as possible so you can tap into emotional, verbal and body language cues.

Be considerate of others' time; keep your emails brief and to the point.

Proofread your emails for clarity, conciseness and completeness.

Emails with typos will lead the reader to question/doubt the accuracy of any subsequent correspondence you have with him.

If it's starting to get complicated, do what winners do: **PICK UP THE PHONE!!**

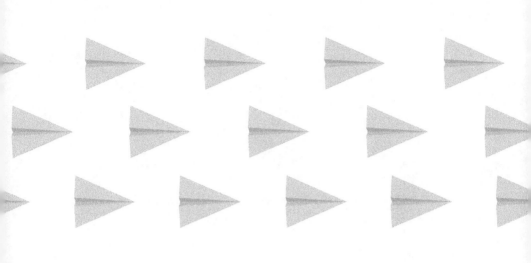

SECTION 3

ON THE "COURT"

"Pretend every single person you meet with has a sign around his or her neck that says, 'Make me feel important.' Not only will you succeed in sales, you will succeed in life."[46]
— Mary Kay Ash

---

[46] blog.markkayfoundation.org.

CHAPTER 8

Game Time – The First Real Conversation

Yes, it's game time and you'd better be on your game. The intensity and pressure is mounting, and you need to bring a heightened sense of focus to everything you say and do during this first meeting. Now, as you sit face to face for the first time with your prospect, you have the opportunity to communicate your personal brand promise – what makes you special, and what differentiates you and your venue from all your competitors. It's a great opportunity, but one fraught with landmines, if you are not careful. Everything you say and do, every eye and hand movement, is conveying something about who you are and what you stand for. Your prospect is absorbing all of it and making some rapid evaluations. The best salespeople have a heightened awareness of this dynamic. They know that – right or wrong – first impressions are extremely difficult to change. So, this is a very important moment for both parties. Since the prospective customer is taking time out of his busy day to meet with you, your chances of booking an event have increased significantly.

By the way, it is always best to confirm an appointment a day or two prior. Whether that be a personal telephone call, an email or text message – you should defer to your prospective customer's preferred method of communication in this regard. Also, determine the most appropriate and/or creative location to meet, again, giving thought to what you think might be the prospective customer's preference or what you think might be the most impressive. The entire communication should be clear, concise, professional and, of course, hospitable.

So, how do you go about handling your first real face-to-face customer conversation? There is a process, of course, and it starts even before the two of you meet.

Prepare to Win

Football Coach Paul "Bear" Bryant once said:

> *"It's not the will to win that matters...it's the will to prepare to win that matters."*[47]

And Basketball Coach John Wooden said:

> *"Failing to prepare is preparing to fail."*[48]

Part of being properly prepared to win is having an agenda. It is not necessarily tightly scripted, but it does need to demonstrate that you are confident, knowledgeable and in control. Are you prepared beyond nervous or fearful? That's where you have to be mentally. The sale is made in your head first.

Your Pre-Game Warm Up

Ask yourself:

- Am I mentally ready and open to doing all that I can to make this customer(s) feel comfortable today?

- Do I have an opening statement that sets the tone for the meeting?

- Am I leaving myself open to establishing that initial "connection" with the customer?

---

[47] Passiton.com
[48] azquotes.com

- Have I prepared some general questions, about the prospect's company or organization?

- Have I taken 15 minutes to review my notes from my first solicitation call, the company's website and/or publications, and anything else I know about the individual(s) I am going to meet?

- Have I prepared specific questions about the buyer?

- Have I prepared some questions about the event itself?

- Am I ready to ask some questions about their current situation at the appropriate time?

- Have I checked the ballroom or meeting space I will be showing today, making sure it is clean and unoccupied?

- Does the receptionist know the names of the guests and what time they will arrive?

- Will I be ready at the end of today's meeting to propose a course of action for next steps?

- Is a nice leather-bound book in the reception area, filled with thank-you letters from delighted customers? Is it easily accessible for them to thumb through while waiting just a few minutes for you to make your entrance? If it is a major appointment, there is nothing wrong with moving one or two of your thank-you letters to the front of the book.

Note: That's correct; keep them waiting…for just a few minutes. It helps your guests settle down a bit and make the mental transition to meeting with you. If the receptionist smiles and greets your guest by name, and if he looks through the letter book, consider it all a bonus for you, in terms of being able to start on an even more positive note.

Note: Be sure to keep the book and any awards your venue has received prominently displayed and current. Even the most glowing letters from 10 years ago are a turn off

Your warm up will pay off big time, in terms of bolstering your self-confidence – setting the stage, so to speak – and launching you into this conversation. This confidence shows through directly to the customer.

What to Home in on: As you move into your first meeting, you'll want to watch out and listen for all the non-verbal communication. Is the guest relaxing in his chair? Is he giving you his full attention? Does he smile more as the meeting progresses? Is his smile a rather cold, polite one or a truly genuine smile? Or is there no smile at all? Does he use your name? Does he ask questions about your venue and/or about you? As he answers your questions, does he give short replies or fuller, more detailed responses? Does he maintain eye contact? Does he take notes? Does he have a good sense of humor? Does he lean closer and have generally warm gestures? Or, does he lean back or look away? Does he speak while you are speaking? Does he fidget and/or is his body tense?

At this point, having a slightly scripted agenda provides you with a mental roadmap and frees you up to observe all that is going on about you. When there is a contradiction between the words and the body language…trust the body language.

FIRST SERVE

1. Do you enter the reception area with folders, brochures and notepad in hand? Or, do you walk into the reception area, hands free, with an open stance and a warm welcome? The latter, of course.

2. Do you further initiate by inviting your guest to step into your conference room?

3. Do you use the guest's name several times and as appropriate? This helps secure his attention, making him start to feel comfortable

and it helps tremendously when you want to make or emphasize a point. Most important: It shows him he is important to you.

4. A word about smiles: Have one. Not the polite, fake kind, but your own authentic smile. Customers have a genuine and emotional response to a real smile.

5. Do you observe where everyone sits at the conference table? This is important, as it gives some indication as to each individual's position and influence within their organization. Simultaneously, do you demonstrate a spirit of hospitality by offering your guest(s) a beverage?

6. Do you then initiate a professional exchange of business cards, looking at each card and each person? The business card exchange shows respect for all in attendance and conveys that all are welcome and included. In certain cultures, the proper exchange of business cards is so important that how it's done can make or break a sale.

7. Do you effectively refocus everyone's attention on the purpose of today's meeting in both word, tone and body language?

It's important to purposely initiate all these actions from the very beginning of the meeting to slow down the sales process. Sadly, this is almost the exact opposite of what many salespeople do. The first benefit of all of this: You are starting – very subtly – to dictate play, by demonstrating that you are prepared, confident and, thus, on offense. The secondary benefit: With this strong foundation, it will be that much easier later on to ask all those provocative, difficult, uncomfortable questions you are going to have to ask.

GAME DYNAMICS

As much as some might think the first meeting is an opportunity to talk a lot, it is not. The first meeting is all about active listening and observation. This will drive all your future actions. Your role today is far more weighted towards getting information than giving it. The more details you watch and listen for about a customer, the more you will stand out from your competition. That's your goal.

To my point, I recently met with a financial advisor for a discussion of my overall finances and future planning. We had scheduled a one-hour meeting. Although this person had never met me before, he immediately talked "at" me for 50 minutes straight about his company and products. I never said a word, nor was I asked to. Then, in the last 10 minutes, he asked me a few questions, mostly about setting up our next appointment and what he would need from me. Although it probably never even crossed his mind, I had mentally left the room about 20 minutes into his "pitch." Do you think he gained a client that day?

Back to our conversation: Want to impress? Don't start off by telling them everything about your venue. Just like in any relationship (think in the context of dating), first look for areas of commonality. You want to first talk about what they are interested in. You want to see where can you connect. People do business with people they like and trust. Simply letting the customer talk, and listening carefully, is the best first step in that direction. People will tend to listen to you if you will listen to them.

Establishing a Connection

In those critical first 10 to 15 minutes of your meeting, you will want to establish some kind of connection with this potential customer. But before you can really do that, you have to focus on getting comfortable with your guest(s). More to the point, you need to make sure he feels comfortable with you. It is the base point from which everything else follows. When this is done correctly, it starts to become apparent to your guest that this is going to be a conversation, not a "sales pitch" or "spiel."

In this preliminary phase of your meeting, look for opportunities early on to pose questions or elicit personal information about them.

For example, if the buyer just returned from a vacation or one of his children just started college, or he just bought a house, say something to the effect of, "That's impressive." Smile warmly and nod your head in an approving manner. It will affirm his sense of pride. If the person you are meeting with says something further in response, let him expand on it, and if you have children of the same age, or have been to the same vacation spot, let him know; it helps establish this very basic and important common ground. If it is about his recent trip, ask where he stayed. What was his favorite part of the trip? What was the food like? All of this helps your prospective customer open up to you more. You are effectively breaking through the daily patter that substitutes for real conversation.

Note: Getting comfortable with a prospective customer can take more or less time, based on several variables. One specific is location. In New York City, you might spend five minutes getting comfortable with someone, but in another area of the country, 10 to 15 minutes would be more the norm. In certain areas of the country, anything less than 15 or 20 minutes, and the customer would be offended by your aggressive approach. In New York, anything more than 10 minutes and the customer is thinking, "Come on! Let's get this show on the road!" It is a matter of getting to a point in the conversation where you sense the customer is relaxed and centered…relaxed enough to be open to moving further along in the conversation.

If you cannot get the individual to start feeling comfortable, then you will have little chance of establishing a connection with him. And as far as establishing that connection, it does not always happen in the same way every time or as quickly as you might be led to believe. It could gradually develop over the course of your meeting and, conceivably, not be fully established until after your appointment. The important thing is to continue to be open to establishing that connection throughout. Although the sooner you can establish this connection the better, the more important point is to not force it. Let it happen and at its own pace.

Your opening comments need to set the overall tone for your meeting. And, your remarks should guide – not control – the meeting. Say, for example:

> *"Thank you for meeting with me today. My objective (or what I would like to do today) is first: to find out what you would like to accomplish by the end of our meeting today. Second, I would like to learn as much as I can about your company (organization or your situation) and this partic-ular event, to determine how best I can be of service to you and your organization. I have a number of questions, and I am sure you have a few for me, as well. It will generally take us about 50 minutes to go through this agenda and site tour. Does that sound alright?"*

Suppose he says he only has 30 minutes. Smile (even laugh a bit – the idea is to keep it light) and say, "Ok, sure, we will go with the edited version today." But what if he says he has less than 30 minutes? My response to that would be: "Wow! That's really not enough time to go through this thoroughly. It really would not benefit either one of us. Can we reschedule for a better date and time that fits into your sched-ule?" That's pretty assertive, even confrontational, but remember, we're still qualifying. In this instance, I don't think the individual(s) has a real interest in doing business with you. He is probably just trying to get a quick price quote to use as leverage against someone else.

Now when, on a few occasions, I found myself in this situation and had no alternative I gave a brief tour. However, when (invariably) the prospective customer insisted on receiving some kind of pricing, I gave an extremely broad price range, and on the high side. If he followed up by asking for a set of menus, I would bring everything to a close by simply stating we would be happy to put together a much more detailed and formal proposal at a later date, once we have met with him or her and any other key decision-makers for a more in-depth discussion. The non-verbal communication, combined with your relaxed and confident demeanor and body language, conveys the message that if this person wants to have a serious conversation, you are ready and, if not, you can just as easily walk away – you don't need this sale and you don't need to waste your time. This is what I was referring to earlier in Chapter 2 when talking about how you put a passive-aggressive Price Hound back on his heels.

If someone cannot commit to even 30 minutes, ask yourself: "Is he really serious? Is this really important to him, or am I just wasting my valuable time?" People will almost always commit the time it takes to do the important things right – if they are serious.

There are two rules of the road when talking about sales in general, first meetings specifically, and price quotes in particular:

> 1. The more you can defer talking about price, the more successful you will be.
> 2. The more trust you have established, the less price will matter.

He who talks price last usually wins. So, when someone sits down with you for that first face-to-face meeting, gracefully deflect that inevitable question as long as possible. Quotes are numbers. Proposals – and that is your goal – are statements of facts and reasons why they should buy from you.

YOUR QUESTIONS

Outlined below are several basic questions you should prepare and consider asking the prospective customer during your first appointment. A lot of salespeople do not engage the customer with enough or the right questions to develop a vivid diagnostic of what their real needs are. I am not suggesting you ask every single question – you pick your questions, based on that sense of touch we have referred to several times before.

About the company:

- I know (state one or two; preferably two things) about your company/organization. What else should I know?
- From what I have seen and read about your organization…you are a leader in your field. I'm sure it was not easy to get to that point… (and then let them finish the sentence).
- How would you describe your company culture?
- What would you say distinguishes your organization from everyone else?
- How long has your organization been hosting this event?

These and similar questions get the ball rolling and tee-up the next and more important questions.

Note: You do not want to start your conversation with a question like, "How's business?' If the answer is terrible, you have placed the conversation in a very deep hole from which it will be very difficult to extract yourself.

About the buyer:

- How long have you been working with your company?
- Where did you work before?
- What other meetings do you plan during the year and how far in advance do you start your planning?
- Have you always been in the same position?
- Do you enjoy planning this event every year?
- Is there anything preventing you from using our facility at this time?
- Can you talk me through the process of how your company selects/evaluates venues for this particular event?
- Is there anyone else involved we need to get information to?
- Who else will need to sign off on this project?

- Will you alone be making the decision as far as changing venues?
- I have worked with other companies (such as yours) that have multiple decision makers. Who, other than yourself, would be involved with the decision-making process?

Although, to a degree, these questions help build your connection with the prospect, the larger purpose of these questions is to find out how this person fits into the buying decision. How much power or influence does he bring to bear on the buying decision?

ABOUT THE EVENT:

While closed-end, transactional questions are the nuts and bolts of the event, and will need to be asked eventually, asking them at the beginning of your meeting is the worst way to start your discussion, though many do. When asked at the onset, these kinds of questions will inhibit discussion and interfere with establishing rapport. They include such questions as:

- How many people will attend?
- What type of meeting room set-up do you need?
- Will you require overnight rooms?
- Will you require audiovisual services?
- Do you prefer a working lunch or buffet, or a three-course sit-down meal in a separate room?
- Will there be any coffee breaks and how many?
- What is your overall budget for this event?
- Is anyone being honored? Will any dignitaries be attending?

When asked too early in the discussion, you will come across as rushed and simply going through the motions – not a good impression! In addition, the staccato rhythm of these types of questions will encourage dry, impersonal answers from your prospect and, before you know it, you've lost any hope at a connection; you are back in "commodity land."

When leading with or focusing exclusively on closed-ended questions, you keep the customer thinking and responding in a transactional mode. He will be skeptical, cautious and generally distrustful. This is a very natural instinct when you have not established a connection.

If you stick with Active-Focused Listening and asking a few open-ended questions at the beginning, when you do get to questions about the event itself, you will gain extremely detailed information back, because at that point, the customer will be much more engaged in the entire process.

About the Current Situation (The Status Quo):

This is the most important part of our conversation today. It is here we talk at length about the status quo. All of these questions are designed to uncover problems, issues and, therefore, opportunities. If you do not uncover the prospect's needs and pain points, you will continue to employ the least productive selling principle – the law of averages. At this juncture, you are stepping up your game and it will all happen naturally, if you let it.

Serve and Volley

- What priorities matter most to you?
- What is the main purpose of the event?
- What will make it a success for you? What's on your wish list?
- What would you say a company has to do to secure your loyalty?
- What would you like to accomplish by the end of our meeting today?
- What venues are you currently using? What are you looking for in a new venue?
- Can you tell me about one or two important outcomes you are looking to achieve as a result of this event?

- If you could organize this event next year – and had free reign – how would you go about it and what would you change?
- How do you handle (using an example of an element in the event which you think our venue excels at) currently?
- How is your current method of handling this element working for you?
- If you could, what is the one thing about last year's event you would change?
- What has held you back from using our venue in the past?
- What is driving your need for change?
- How do you see the event flowing?
- How do you see us helping you with this? What are you hoping we could do for you?
- What would you say are the top three goals for this event?

As you uncover needs, but especially specific pain points, make sure you convey by your facial expression, tone of voice and pace of conversation that you understand the seriousness of these issues. You want to probe deeper and you show that by physically moving closer and asking the prospect to expand on these issues. You…

MOVE TO NET

- How long have you had this problem?
- Can you tell me a little bit more about that?
- I'm not sure I fully understand…can you help me…and tell me a little bit more about (some particular item) specifically?
- Have you had some other experiences that led to that concern?
- Have you tried to fix it in the past?
- What impact does this particular problem have on you, specifically?
- If this situation continues, what kind of impact do you think it could have in the future?

The Smile Question: Here is a very effective question I often used as I came to "net." Maintain a positive, friendly tone – smile when you ask: "Is there anything about your relationship with the facility you are currently using (or is there anything about last year's event) you would change if you could?" Once you have asked this question, you need to shut up and wait for an answer. If the answer is "nothing," you need to look right at them and say, "I'm confused; where did I lose you?" He may look a bit confused too, but the point of the matter is if there is nothing he would change, then why are we even meeting today? He has to come back to you with a reason to be there. If everything is fine, then shouldn't he just rebook the venue he was with last year? If you find yourself in this situation, there's nothing wrong with posing this question: "I have to assume when we arranged our appointment you were looking to find something better than what you have now. Based on your answers to the questions I have already asked, I think we probably do. However, when we get to this point, and you say no, it would really be helpful to know exactly where I lost you? " Again, just shut up, stop talking. Great salespeople know their job is to convey they are honest, open, non-threatening and professional. In a relaxed conversational tone, they pose questions and then simply wait for the answers.

"A Light Touch"

Assuming the prospective customer answers your "smile question" on the first try, the skilled salesperson can then gently introduce one or two of his own thoughts about the event, drawing on his own deep knowledge and experience. For example: "You know, I worked with an organization once that had a similar issue or concern. This is what we did to address that issue, and they found it to be very successful." At this point, because the salesperson has taken all the steps, asked all the pertinent questions outlined in this chapter, and established some kind of connection with the prospect, his comments are usually well received. Because his comments and relaxed demeanor are both professional, candid and down to earth, his remarks bear more weight and his own personal knowledge and experience even further supports this premise.

The salesperson's comments flow logically from being a strong listener, and this is not lost on the prospective customer. What's also not lost on the customer is …there's no pressure.

You can further impact the situation by specifically naming the organization you worked with; it implies the customer could check/verify your statement directly and yet you are not pushing them to do so. In essence you will have actually posed a "trial buying statement." It is extremely subtle. Trial buying and closing questions/statements will be reviewed shortly in Chapter 10. A good point to remember at this point, however, is that great salespeople pose these questions much, much earlier in the sales process than do their counterparts.

THE SITE VISIT

A site inspection is usually part of the first meeting, though it should not be the first part. After you have had your initial fact-finding discussion and developed a shared vision of the event, you are ready to show off your facilities. Like everything else, the key to a good site inspection is good preparation and anticipation. The "choreography and orchestration" of a good site visit includes:

A. **Staging.** Make sure you've walked through the area you will be showing so there are no surprises. If you want the ballroom walls all opened up, make sure they are opened. See what's around you in your venue that day. If a group similar to the prospect's organization is meeting in your facility today, it can be helpful for them to see it "in action."

B. **Selecting Co-stars.** The prospect – the potential buyer – is the star. You decide who – if anyone else – is going to co-star today. For example: The executive chef (if food is a main focus), or your general manager (if your prospect is particularly status-conscious). Use co-stars sparingly, if at all. And, be careful not to let the co-stars dominate the discussion and/or upstage the star.

C. **Mirroring.** Research shows waiters improve their tips simply by repeating back word for word what the customer ordered. Model and match ("mirror") the speech, tone, volume, vocabulary, clothes and movement of the potential customer. In general, if you are meeting with a law firm, dress more conservatively. If you're meeting with a fashion organization, less so. If the client talks quickly, talk quickly. If they talk slowly, talk slowly. Mirroring makes people feel comfortable. When you repeat back what someone says it shows you heard, you understand, and that you and the prospect are on the same page. Similarly, with dress, we are most comfortable with people who appear to be like us.

D. **Sitting Him Down.** Many salespeople simply meet a guest in the reception area and immediately take him for a tour of the facility. This plays right into the mindset that a catering event, the facility and the salesperson, too, are just commodities. What you will always want to do is get them re-focused and engaged in a conversation first; then you take them for a walk. Your walk-through will then have some sense of a shared vision. Otherwise, it is just a data collection exercise.

E. **Getting Him Up.** Well you got him to sit down, but don't forget to then get him back up for a tour. Get him "actively" involved in reviewing your facility. This further goes to helping him more strongly consider your venue. Keep in mind, if he doesn't want to tour the facility, that says something. In that case, it could be time to ask an uncomfortable question, such as, "What is your real interest in us?" Or "Why don't you want to see the meeting space?"

F. **Showing Energy and Enthusiasm.** It's your job to have energy and enthusiasm, even if you don't feel it. It may be your 2,000[th] time doing a walkthrough of the facility, but it may your prospect's first time.

G. **Encourage Imagining.** Help the customer start experiencing the meeting space as theirs. For example, if a potential customer plans for a number of silent-auction tables plus several registration tables, show him where you would suggest placing the tables and almost mimic where you would place them. Encourage him to walk on the Grand Ballroom stage so he can imagine himself in the venue. The more the prospect is walking around and envisioning his event, the more he is committing to booking the event with you. This is a clear buying signal. If you cannot initiate or encourage this kind of imagining, it's time for some difficult, uncomfortable questions, such as: "Where did I lose you? I'm sensing something may be wrong."

H. **Performing.** There is a world of difference between letting someone take a look at the Grand Ballroom and presenting the Grand Ballroom. It's called "showmanship." Your gestures, mannerisms and energy level should fill the space. This will help the prospect start to envision how the ballroom will work to their advantage.

Note: Only use this technique during the site visit. In the initial meeting room discussion, do just the opposite.

Good salespeople "lead" the prospect into the ballroom. They are confident, at ease and "on" as required. In tennis lingo, they dictate points. They introduce points from their prior discussion that reflect how the facility accommodates and/or better serves those points. They are not pushing, but they are probing. They also don't passively let the prospective customer wander around and look at the space at their own pace. The former approach shows you are in control of "play"; the latter will cause your prospect to wonder if you are even in the game.

CONFIRMING NEXT STEPS: A MUTUAL DECISION

Sometimes the next step is setting up a second meeting to review the facility with any other decision-makers (such as the parents of the bridal couple or the president of the association). Other times the logical next step is a request for a formal proposal. Now, assuming the prospective customer has not said anything at all about next steps, you can conclude your first meeting by simply thanking your potential customer for taking time out of his busy schedule to visit with you. Tell him you learned quite a bit about him, his organization and their event, and then ask directly: "How would you like to proceed?" Best case, the prospective customer will ask you to prepare a formal proposal. If, however, he would like to "get with a few other people and come back to you" to set up another appointment, a good response would be, "Of course, I understand. Why don't I give you a call, say next Wednesday, once you have had a chance to get everybody together on your end?" This is all based on your having a good positive gut reaction about the person. You then shut up and wait. If he is being forthright, he will agree to this plan or quickly propose an alternate date. If there is some hesitation though, then you need to ask: "It sounds like (or it seems like) there is some hesitation here – can you help me? Is there something I have missed or that we need to discuss further?" (Again; smile and stay relaxed).

It's always best for the prospect to ask you to present a proposal, but alternatively you might say: "I would like to review everything I have learned today and put together some cost calculations. Then, with your permission, I'd like to submit a formal proposal outlining exactly how we can improve upon your current situation (or meet your expectations/make your event a success)." By now, the prospective customer has learned that you are not the "typical" salesperson – immediately talking price and logistics and/or bringing a cast of thousands to your meeting, or making those horrible comments that assume the customer will be hosting the event with you. This prospect is starting to actually trust that you are different and so, maybe, you are better. "Different" is extremely good in sales.

This is why having a face-to-face meeting is so important. You cannot have a deep sense of who the potential customer truly is by email or even by telephone. The same applies to those who subscribe to having several unnecessary people (for example, department heads) join them on their appointments. How do you possibly get to the level of this more intense, personal communication with the sheer distraction of all of those other people being there?

Extend Yourself One More Time

The very last thing I say at the end of any meeting is, "Is there anything else I can do for you today?" It is a nice, thoughtful and memorable way to conclude. It shows your guests that you are a true professional and that you know what your role is in this relationship. And, it is another one of those little things that differentiate you from your competition. For the also rans, this never even crosses their minds.

On the Spot Self-Critique

Debrief after every appointment (but especially after a major site visit). Go through everything while it is still fresh in your mind. Ask yourself: Did I cover everything? Did I sense confirmation on all the major points? If not, which ones and what immediate next steps will I take to correct that? What areas did not go as well as expected and why? What did I discover today, and does it have sales implications to move this prospect forward? What did I discover today that might lead to our losing the game on this one? What are some of the key takeaways for me about them and their event? You can learn so much from these "self-critiques" and it can improve your performance so much the next time you step on the "court."

TAKEAWAYS:

Your physical body language flows from your level of certainty.

Your level of certainty flows from how well prepared you are.

Breathe from your diaphragm — it slows your breathing, pace and speech. It also helps to overcome nervousness, and it instills confidence and calmness.

Do not smile too quickly. It can seem insincere and inauthentic. A gradual smile indicates you are genuine and in the moment. The same with your eyebrows. Raised slightly, this helps establish your approachability.

Don't come into a meeting with an already fully prepared proposal and, worse, present it almost immediately to the customer. (You think I'm kidding? I've seen it happen!)

Don't say things like "actually" or "honestly" — you are implying that up until now, you have been lying.

Avoid unnecessary and weak words, such as "just," "sort of," "perhaps," "probably," "I guess" and "we might." They undercut your confidence and authority.

Avoid jargon, buzzwords and corporate speak — they are "Trust Busters."

Swing Thought: *Throughout the meeting/site visit, ask yourself, "What's the thing that differentiates me from all other salespeople?" It will non-verbally translate to your prospective customer.*

To be persuasive we must be believable; to be believable
we must be credible; to be credible we must be truthful."[49]
– Edward R. Murrow

---
[49] Famousquotes.com

CHAPTER 9

The Proposal – Why You Should Buy from Me

This is the heart of it, the core of what we do: Submit proposals only to "true" prospective customers. Professional salespeople do not make "pitches," they make presentations. They present proposals personalized around the stated needs, wants, objectives and budgetary guidelines articulated to them by their prospective customers.

As with prospecting and solicitation, the same guideline applies to proposals: The more face-to-face meetings and site presentations you do, the more proposals you will be asked to generate. The more proposals you present, ultimately, the more sales you will secure. Similar to your solicitation letters, you want to send your proposals to decision makers or, at a minimum, to key influencers. Otherwise, you are in an extremely weak position as you move into the next critical stage.

As you consider your proposal, your guiding thought should be to provide the prospect with a focused, detailed plan that solves a problem, relieves pain, adds value and/or provides an easier way of executing their event. In other words, you want to present him with an opportunity for a noticeable improvement over his current or alternative situation. You need to show you can solve problems and solve them better than your competitors, and deliver the best, most successful event for him. Let's review a few proposals with an eye to how the sales manager set themselves up for failure.

Note: As you will see there are no specific menus included in the proposals to follow. I have done that for two reasons. First, for proprietary reasons and second, because the menu in itself is really almost secondary to all that surrounds it. This should become clearer as we move along through this section. I have, however, included a much fuller formatted menu proposal (for reference) further along in this chapter.

EXAMPLE 1: POLITICAL PARTY ELECTION NIGHT PARTY

I referred this lead to a salesperson at one of our properties, explaining who the prospective customer was, his needs and his limited budget, which is fairly typical for an election night event. Around 90% of the time, political groups keep these events pretty bare bones – sandwiches, chips and a cash bar. At most, they may include a hosted beer and wine bar. The result:12 pages of emails with questions, statistics etc., and a 10-page full-color proposal outlining "various" options for food and beverage. The customer's budget was $10-15K maximum. The proposal was $45-55K – just about three times (300% over) the stated budget, and way more than they were able to spend. Was the salesperson listening at all to either one of us?

EXAMPLE 2: PROPOSAL FOR A WEDDING (EMAIL)

Hello Cathy Shay

We are delighted you are considering our venue for your event. Our venue is the ideal location, centrally located (blah...blah...).

We are proposing our newly renovated and elegant Imperial Ballroom (blah...blah...) creative space; it is the perfect location for an impressive dinner event.

For a true experience, we are also suggesting our (blah...blah...blah....). We know each one of your attendees will be ecstatic about the exceptional service and delectable cuisine. Please see our attached link to photos. Special occasion menus can be found under the catering drop-down.

Our pricing proposal would be $145 pp for all reception and dinner food; $50 pp for a five-hour open bar, or $12.00 *per drink on consumption. Pricing is based on a minimum guarantee of 700 guests with a food and beverage minimum of $136,500.*

Bartender fees of $＿＿ would apply.

Coatroom fees of $＿＿ per person would apply.

Electrical fees based on entertainment requirements would apply.

<u>Concessions</u>: Complimentary choice of linen color, complimentary votive candles, dance floor, stage, tables and chairs. And, finally, a dedicated hotel event planner to assist you in planning a flawless event.

As of now, I am not holding space for your program. Please let me know if you would like me to place the space on a tentative hold until you have made a decision. If space is confirmed as available, I would be happy to quickly prepare a contract for you.

Allow us the opportunity to exceed your expectations with our vast experience and excellent customer service. Our staff looks forward to introducing you to the superior hospitality upon which we have built our reputation of excellence. We understand you will consider several factors during your venue selection process, but we are confident that our venue will complement your needs perfectly. I look forward to hearing from you.

Mistakes:

- "Hello Cathy Shay"– indicates a computer-generated form letter. How about "Dear Cathy"?
- "Your event"? It's her wedding! The most important day in her life!
- The next several paragraphs are full of all the usual overhyped venue descriptors, with no connection to nor attempt to address needs and wants and, therefore, values. All features... no benefits!

- The photos link is an excellent visual for the customer. The statement about the menu link, however, comes across as generic and impersonal. A typewritten formal menu would be much more personal and probably much easier to access.
- "Price Summary" is misleading, and since the customer's guests are extremely light drinkers (for religious and cultural reasons), why would you propose open bar pricing when, clearly, they should be offered per drink pricing. Yes, you did offer a per drink price, but the catering minimum guarantee is based on a full open bar at $195 per person for a total of $136,500. At this point the customer cannot help but question your integrity.
- No low, middle and upper price points were offered.
- Concessions? You are going to graciously give me stuff everybody else provides for free? I don't get it.
- You are going to give me a dedicated event planner? You mean if I book my wedding with you, you are then going to hand me over to someone else? And is this really a concession? After all, the venue assigns an event planner to every event they book, right?
- "…quickly prepare a contract?" Most customers actually want you to take your time when preparing a contract; they want you to give it a lot of thought and careful analysis.
- "As of now I am not holding space for your program." Again, you still haven't figured out my "program" is my wedding?
- "If space is confirmed as available…." You mean you are still deciding if you want to host my wedding or not? Well, excuse me! The most important perception a salesperson can convey is that they will make it happen for a customer. Does this statement contribute to that perception?
- The first two sentences in the very last paragraph are all too typical. It makes that huge assumption the prospective customer will, of course, be selecting this venue for their event. Customers find this off-putting and egotistical, and it definitely does not lend itself to building trust.
- And finally: "During your venue selection process…." This is kind of a cold, sterile type of statement to make, particularly

to a person planning her wedding. I might see it as more applicable to a corporate meeting planner.

- I look forward to hearing from you." Your last statement to a potential customer should be a very clear and specific notation of what you will do next after this proposal has been sent. It should also be a call to action. Shouldn't you be calling her? Shouldn't you be demonstrating a sincere desire to work with her on this important event in her life?

Here's one from a slightly different angle:

EXAMPLE 3: AN ANNUAL REPEAT CUSTOMER (EMAIL)

"This is Mr. X, here at the XXX. I believe I handled your group last year and will once again do the same this year. I currently have your proposal ready which is simply a copy/paste from last year's production.

Please contact me at your earliest convenience to discuss further—xxx-xxx-xxxx.

We look forward to ensuring the absolute success of your program!

Kindest Regards,"

MISTAKES:

- It must be comforting for the customer, who spends 60/70% of his day planning this event, to know this is simply a "copy and paste" from last year.
- The manager compounds the issue by saying he believes he handled their group last year. You mean he doesn't know?
- Handled? Your group? Sounds like trucking company terms. How about "…had the pleasure of serving (name of organization)."
- Since this manager did work with the customer last year, wouldn't picking up the phone and welcoming him back be a bit more engaging? Relationship or…transaction?

Here's a proposal for a major event. This template can be used for just about any event. It would, of course, be abbreviated based on the size and scope of the particular event. Obviously, you would add in detailed descriptions of all food and beverage offered, keeping in mind that the menu should reflect the audience, be seasonal and appropriate to the occasion. All food descriptions should be clear and concise.

Proposal
Especially prepared for
The XYZ Foundation
15th Anniversary Gala
Thursday, November 15, 2013
(insert Organization Logo)

Reception 6:00pm to 7:00pm
Dinner 7:00pm -9:00pm
Dancing until 11:00pm

Reception (one hour)

<u>Butler Passed</u>
White Wine, Champagne and Sparkling Water during reception.

Specify all brands of liquor, beer, wine and
sodas being served on all bars.

We will include one (1) Specialty Drink for the evening (exact drink to be determined). We will have a table tent on each bar highlighting and promoting the drink.

An Elegant Array of Butler-Passed Hors d'oeuvres and Canapés
(6 pieces per person)

Hot Hors d'oeuvres
Specify 3 items

Cold Selections
Specify 3 items

Note: If there are stations, list as well, with a notation if an attendant is required.

DINNER

Appetizer
Specify three items

Entree
Specify three different entrees (beef, poultry, lamb)

Dessert
Specify three items
Confections
Coffee, Tea, Decaffeinated Coffee

Wine Service with Dinner
Specify names of wine (how many bottles per table, or
how long wine service will be. (e.g., 1 ½ hours).

Beverage-Dinner (4 hours) – if required
Specify all liquor, wine, beers and sodas being served on bars.

PRICING SUMMARY (PER PERSON)

$160 with Chicken Chasseur entrée
$170 with Filet Mignon entrée
$184 with Rack of Lamb entrée

This price includes:

- All reception food as outlined for one hour
- All reception beverage as outlined for one hour
- All dinner food as outlined
- All wine service with dinner for one and a half hours

Set up time of the Grand Ballroom to be from 2 pm-on.
Exclusive use of entire floor – no other event on the floor.

Note: All pricing is based upon a catering minimum guarantee of X guests @ $ ____ per person, and a total catering revenue of $____, exclusive of XX % service charge and XX % tax.

This price does not include:

- Coat check fees of $____per person, based on the minimum guarantee or the final guarantee –whichever is higher.
- Bartender fees of $____for each of (x) bartenders and station attendant fees of $____ for (x) attendants.
- All beverage service for [4] additional hours (optional) at $ ____ per person.
- Audio, Visual, Electrical, Music, Flowers, Photography Services.
- __% Service Charge on any additional food and beverage purchases.
- ____% sales tax on additional items – organization is tax exempt.
- Accent lighting on all dinner tables @ $____.
- Custom linens @ $____ and up, per cloth, depending on style.

ENHANCEMENTS

In addition, we will provide the following enhancements on a complimentary basis:

- An office for your use on a complimentary basis for the entire day.
- Complimentary lighting gobos at each of the main entrances of our venue with the XX logo.
- Greeters on arrival to assist in directing your guests to coat check and registration.
- One (1) complimentary suite for the night of your event.
- Advance Alert System – that allows you to request, respond to and connect in real time to our venue's operational staff, assuring faster resolution of all requests.

Your Team

Outlined below is the team that will work with you on a daily basis to execute and ensure a great event:

Director of Catering Sales (name)_____
Director of Event Management (name)_____
Overnight Guest Room Coordinator (name)_____
Director of Audiovisual Services (name)_____
Executive Chef (name)_____
Director of Banquets (name)_____
Director of Event Services (name) _____
Hospitality Suite Manager (name)_____
Executive Pastry Chef (name)_____
Director of Security (for VIPs) _____
Director of Guest Relations (name)_____

Note: The menu outlined above is a suggestion. Final menu selection will be coordinated when we conduct a tasting for this event with our Executive Chef.

- -

Granted, this proposal is quite extensive. In many cases, you would submit a more abbreviated version. Every proposal is different (as is every customer) and needs to be tailored to the customer, based on the size, scope and total revenue of the event. Even the personality of the customer should be taken into consideration. Some key items, however, stand out in this particular proposal, which can be incorporated into just about any proposal:

- The very first line says, "Especially Prepared for…." It is saying this proposal is not some "canned" standard boilerplate proposal. It is special and specific to you.
- A logo of the organization on the first page helps to further personalize – differentiate – the proposal.
- The menu is presented in an easy to understand/read format. It is well-spaced and in chronological order.
- It is very specific. It specifies the exact brands to be served at the reception and the names of the wines to be served with dinner, as well as the quantity and time specifications for service. It further notes butler passed wine, champagne and mineral waters at the reception.
- There is – purposefully – a limited number of menu options. Less is decidedly more when it comes to menus. Proposals should offer only a few options (3 max). Many venues send proposals with 15 different entrees and 35 different hors d'oeuvres. It is too much and too confusing. We live in a society that inundates you with information, choices and alternatives. People want to simplify their lives; help them. Otherwise, they might just shut down and make no decision at all.
- The price summary is concise and very easy to read; it details everything that is included and not included in the price.
- In short, this proposal is very direct and transparent; it does not leave anything to chance or misinterpretation.

Note: When you offer three price points, the tendency is for people to select the middle option. It is always best to present what you think is the best option as the mid-point.

Depending on the event and your prospective customer, you may want to add a second page of enhancements, outlining no more than two additional food and beverage options (with costs) for the cocktail party and/or other upgraded appetizer/dessert course options. Internally, we call these "upsells," but with our customer we refer to them as "enhancements." They are the bells and whistles that are nice to have but not absolutely essential. In essence, you are planting the seed for a later conversation. Particularly with weddings, your probability of securing enhancement upsells is very good. The best way to achieve this is to offer it now (six to nine months in advance) – not four weeks before the wedding.

To further personalize your proposal and help your prospect visualize the event, you may want to attach a few photos and diagrams of the event space, set up as the customer would like. Depending on the account, you may also need to include a page of references/testimonial letters from other similarly prestigious organizations or corporations that have used your facility and/or groups that are similar in nature, size or scope. If one or two of those groups have given you permission to give out their name and contact information, indicate that in the proposal and suggest your prospective customer contact them directly regarding their experience with you and your venue. Testimonials can help tremendously in gaining trust, especially with prospects who have had a bad experience. They are also one of the most effective weapons to either overcome or prevent objections and best your competition.

Some salespeople mistakenly lead with testimonial letters they are most proud of, versus those that mirror their prospective customer. This goes to the idea people are most persuaded by people who are similar to themselves. Think of a testimonial as someone (their words) who has found you, through direct experience, to be trustworthy. That's priceless!

Bonus! Are you competing for an annual event that has been at a specific venue for a number of years? If you have a testimonial letter from a similar organization that had been at the same venue and "made the switch" to you – Wow! You just served up an ace right down the "T," as we say in tennis.

Lastly, by listing the names of all members of the team (perhaps even with a brief bio and their qualifications, if the event merits it) you further support the overriding message that you have a sizeable lineup of professionals at your disposal to handle every single aspect of this event. It demonstrates you take this very seriously, that you execute as a team and that you are the leader of that team. You are taking ownership of this operation. This shows your continuing attention to detail, reflects pride in your team, and brings the team to life. For the most part, your competition is not doing this at all, so this is another little thing you can do to distinguish yourself from the "also rans." Will this impress your prospect? Absolutely! And that is the intent.

THE TAKEN-FOR-GRANTED COVER LETTER

Proposals – and specifically, the accompanying cover letter – ideally tee-up the closing and negotiating phase of a sale. Many salespeople make the mistake of proposing "their solution," not necessarily the right solution. It all goes back to offering real and better value, real solutions to real problems/pain, and noticeable improvements over the customer's current situation. The cover letter is where you state your case. This is where you want to play the game.

So many though, overlook or give short shrift to their proposal cover letter. And yet, it is probably the most important part of a strong proposal. Your "Joe Average" salesperson slaps a corporate form letter onto the proposal and calls it a day. For example:

> *Dear Barbara …I am pleased to confirm I am holding the Laguna Ballroom on your preferred dates. I have attached a proposal highlighting a sample menu. I am confident we will exceed your expectations at every turn. From our Executive Chef and Culinary Team, to our impeccable co-ordination by our Event Management Team, you will know you made the right decision in selecting us. If I can answer any questions, please do not hesitate to contact me directly. I do know choosing a venue for your program is a very important decision. We have one of the most prestigious venues*

in the city with world class service and luxurious ballrooms (blah... blah... blah...). I look forward to speaking with and being of personal service to you soon.

Here is another proposal cover letter that is so painfully wrong, yet unfortunately much more common than you might think:

Hi Mr., X. It was a pleasure meeting with you today about your Annual Fundraising Dinner. I have attached a proposal for your review. The proposal indicates a sample menu with the pricing for the full menu. I have reduced the entrée pricing to become competitive with the X Venue. I will continue to hold the Ballroom on November 16 until I hear from you. Please let me know if you have any questions. I look forward to hearing from you. Once again, thank you for your consideration.

What do these two letters have in common?

- Both letters are tedious and reflect a lack of engagement.
- "We are sure to exceed your expectations at every turn," is not impactful; it comes across as "fluff."
- "Impeccable coordination by our event management team...." – it's all just words; it has no meaning for the customer.
- "You know you will have made the right decision in selecting us." This is just not believable!
- In the second letter, in particular: Classic dates, rates, space selling, and even lowering the price to be competitive with an inferior competitor?
- Oh, and "I will continue to hold our Ballroom..." "...until I hear from you." *Are you kidding me?* The concept of building buying pressure, based on supply and demand, apparently was not considered.

- Not personalized (sample menu in both letters) and no real reference in either letter to actually having met with the customers or thanking them for considering us for a $150K event.

Note: Both potential customers got sample menus. My prospective customer "received a proposal" specially prepared for him. The latter goes to the concept of doing the little things, and it shines through in the salesperson's attitude from the very beginning.

- Neither letter reflected a compelling statement of benefits, nor a value proposition as to what the real advantages are of hosting the event with this venue.
- "If you have any questions…you can call me"? Very, very weak.
- The first letter in particular uses language almost assuming the prospective customer will buy. People don't like that. It reflects lack of authenticity and a certain self-centered pride.

Neither of the events booked, and when questioned about them, the salespeople involved didn't know why. They seemed to be straining to even recall the names of the customers and the groups, and that points to salespeople who are not engaged and who are on autopilot.

I once reviewed a proposal with a cover letter that included the following:

- *If I understand you correctly, location is important to you… (blah…blah…blah.)*
- *If I understand you correctly, adequate meeting space is important to you… (blah…blah…blah.)*
- *If I understand you correctly, having different food and beverage options is important to you… (blah…blah…blah.)*

I could understand saying the lead-in once, but three times? The customer is thinking, "What is wrong with this person? The "blah…blah…blah after each bullet point was actually a regurgitation of a lot of generalized corporate speak that was already outlined in the venue's brochures. It falls flat every time, because it is not based on the conversation.

Other disconnects I have observed are letters with statements such as "first draft contract." My first reaction is you are telegraphing a message to the customer that you will negotiate the price. Another disconnect --"Unfortunately, despite my best efforts, we are unable to make any further reductions in pricing." You never want to put yourself in this position .You are indicating you are not in charge and if I were the customer I would ask to speak to whomever is in charge. And; I have also seen --"As you know, our food, service and ambiance greatly exceed what you have had at other venues." From my vantage point you just insulted the customer and have invited a pretty significant backlash.

The "Five Whys"

Your proposal cover letter speaks for you, framing the key issues and providing a mutual roadmap for all subsequent conversation. It has to be a compelling statement of benefits that clearly spells out your value proposition and addresses the prospect's stated and even, on occasion, unstated needs. You have to agree on these very basic points before a customer can make a final decision. Often in the excitement/rush of being asked to submit a proposal, some salespeople overlook the most basic of all concerns that a potential customer is sorting out in his own mind:

- Why change at all?
- Why change now?
- Why spend the money?
- Why choose your solutions and venue over any other?
- Why should I take a chance on you?

Think of these "Five Whys" as football goalposts. Everything you are about to propose to the prospective customer must pass through those goalposts. Winning salespeople make sure their cover letters more than satisfactorily answer all of these questions.

The Preferred Cover Letter

Good proposal cover letters – cover letters that sell – open with an expression of appreciation for the opportunity to meet with the customer. The cover letter then demonstrates an understanding of the key components (based on mutually agreed needs) that you want to emphasize one last time in writing. This is a great opportunity to state your key solutions to those needs. You'll want to state the tangible things they will get ("What's in it for me?") if they decide to book with you; for example: Increased attendance and/or more bottom-line revenue for the charity. The more detailed and personalized your cover letter is, the more sales you will make. Keep in mind, in most cases, your prospect will read the cover letter before the proposal itself. This is your time to shine. Your cover letter should frame the issues, as well as the pursuant conversation. You want to sound both knowledgeable and professional about the customer's needs and about your solution to those needs. This letter (your vision statement) also must reinforce the values and the pain points as addressed in the proposal itself. Your cover letter may be the very last communication you have with the prospect, so you will definitely want it to be a "personal call to action." Let's take a look at the following example. This cover letter was sent to the Executive Director for a major fundraising gala:

> *Dear Ms X,*
>
> *It was a pleasure meeting with you and your Board of Directors recently, regarding the XX Foundation Annual Awards Gala. I appreciate and thank you for the considerable time and attention everyone gave to personally reviewing our facilities with me.*
>
> *As discussed, I have attached a brief but detailed proposal for your further review and consideration. Based upon our meeting and discussion the other day, there are several (or a few) points I would like to reiterate (or highlight):*
>
> *Our large, square-shaped ballroom with a large built-in stage and perfectly balanced and spacious table placement*

allows for greater attendance than you have had in the past, plus your guests can much more easily move about the ballroom than in prior years. This ensures greater flexibility, in terms of accommodating more guests for the event itself, and greater comfort/satisfaction for those attending.

You will now have the ability to place more tables (than in prior years) directly in front of the stage. This opens up the possibility of tiered pricing for the better tables. If nothing else, key table purchasers – those who in the past were fairly removed from the staging area itself – would now be placed in a location more in keeping with their true financial contribution. Wouldn't it be wonderful to enhance their experience with a front row seat?

The Presidential Suite *is a great opportunity for a pre- or post-gala reception event for key donors, honorees and Board members. It's a wonderful marketing opportunity, as well, for XXX Foundation to nurture key relationships and, therefore, increase future contributions to the foundation.*

Silent Auction. *Again, this goes to the point of our greater size, affording you greater flexibility, much greater visibility and – most important – easier access than in the past for all of your guests. This will result in greater audience involvement/engagement and will further translate into increased sales and additional revenue for the foundation.*

(Name), I will call you in a few days, once you have had a chance to review this material. At that time, I would be happy to answer any questions you might have and/or provide you with any other information you may require before all concerned make a final decision regarding the site of this important event.

(Name), I look forward to speaking with you further as to how (name of venue) might hopefully best serve the needs of the XXX Foundation in 2015 and beyond.

Until then I remain

Sincerely,

For a simpler proposal I might opt to send a more customary letter, such as this:

> *Dear Susan;*
>
> *It certainly was a pleasure meeting with you the other day. I appreciate the considerable time you and your colleagues spent personally reviewing our facilities with me.*
> *As discussed, I have attached a brief but detailed proposal for your further consideration.*
>
> ***Note:*** *Here, I might insert one or two short bullet points relating to key needs of the customer, if I thought appropriate.*
>
> *Susan, I will call you in a few days once you have had a chance to review this material. At that time, I would be glad to answer any questions you might have and/or provide you with any other information you may require before all concerned make a final decision regarding this event.*
> *Susan, thank you again and I look forward to speaking with you further as to how (name of facility) might hopefully best serve the needs of (name of organization) this coming October.*
> *Sincerely,*

KEEPS YOU IN THE GAME

You will note in the second to last paragraph of both letters some extremely important words: "I will call you in a few days, at which time I would be happy to answer any other questions you might have and/or provide you with any other information you may require before all concerned make a final decision regarding the site of this event." Why put this in the letter? Because you don't want to take anything for granted. Such language:

- **Lets your prospect know you will be calling in a few days** and, when you do, you have once again fulfilled another promise.
- **Assures your prospect that you are going to make her feel comfortable**, by committing to find out if she has any other questions and/or needs any other information. You are telling her you are there to assist. People can tell when they are dealing with a strong salesperson. They also like to buy from people like that.
- **Confirms you are professional and caring.** People like people who want to help them. They also like to buy from people like that.
- **Gives you a bit of protection.** It's implied that you might make changes to the proposal, based on any new information, prior to them or their Board making a final decision. You are showing that you have an open mind.
- **"…might hopefully best serve….** This is a small point, but I think it resonates with prospects. The statement makes it clear who the boss is, who is making the decision: The customer. So many cover letters try to assume the prospect will be selecting them. The best salespeople never make these assumptions. These four words convey the salesperson's humility, sincerity and their keen awareness they are here to serve. If you are in the hospitality business, you'd better embrace "serving people" – that's what it's all about.

Dealing with Intermediaries

When dealing with intermediaries (regardless if they meet with you directly or if everything is via email and telephone), it is not uncommon for them to say they cannot reveal the name of the client, but they still want you to submit a proposal for the event with "all charges" outlined. You have the responsibility to both yourself and your company to push back on this. My response would be, "I cannot submit a proposal to you at this time." That response is usually greeted with annoyance. That's okay, the intermediary is not the customer. I further explain we are a large company with hundreds of salespeople assigned to every imaginable account. We can be counted on to keep the information confidential, but we really do need to know the customer's name and company so the correct salesperson can interact with him moving forward. After all, why would I want to go through all the work of putting together a proposal, only to find out late in the game the account belongs to another salesperson? When properly explained, I have never had an intermediary decline to give me the name of the account.

A huge and classic mistake many salespeople make is agreeing to submit a proposal after a very brief meeting or after a very brief telephone conversation. They don't challenge the customer (in this case, the intermediary), and press for a more comprehensive meeting first. This is all rooted in fear and a certain amount of just doing what is most comfortable and least stressful for the salesperson. A statement that can be helpful to counter this is: "Usually, we prefer to meet directly with you and any other decision-makers for an in-depth discussion of your needs and budgetary guidelines for your event. Then, based on that information, we can submit a much more detailed and intelligent proposal."

A second point about intermediaries: Do you really expect an organization to make a final decision about a $200K event by email? You have to determine if the intermediary you are corresponding with is a key influencer. From the outset, you should – in a polite way—challenge any intermediary to establish who they are and how they fit into the buying decision.

I have worked with some wonderful intermediaries who partnered with me in our securing events. And, on a few occasions, I have worked with intermediaries who do what I call, "The RFP email blast to the world," and were clearly not open to nor working as my partner. We talk about commoditized customers…the same applies in intermediary situations.

Wait a Minute…What Does it Really Cost??

Note: What follows would apply to only a small number of prospects and only for some very specific reasons. In all other cases, general pricing guidelines would apply.

A word on cost when putting together your initial proposal and when you expect you will soon be entering an intense negotiation: What is the true cost of a dinner menu when your venue is already serving 900 luncheons (with the exact same menu that day) and you are trying to book an event for 600 with the exact same menu that evening? Is the cost really the same? What is the cost if you have sold the ballroom for dinners for an entire week and one date is still open? What profit margin do you have to make to sell that one date? What profit margin will you accept making to sell that date? What if the call for that date was six months out? What if the calls were three months out? What if the call was one month out? Is the cost the same for an event for 1,400 people as it is for 250 people? Particularly with coffee breaks, there can be some built-in high-cost items. The same applies with cuts of beef/poultry and portion size. Sometimes when you do that kind of analysis, you find your price point has a little more flex, so you can reduce price because you have reduced cost.

Takeaways:

Powerful proposals address values and pain points. In the first case, they add to, maintain or enhance them; in the second, they reduce or eliminate them. These are the linchpins of a powerful proposal.

Proposals need to be written and formatted in such a way that the customer can clearly see how you are helping him achieve a goal.

If you don't want to be a participant in the due-diligence charade or, the more likely "Price Hound run around," get an appointment for a site visit before you submit your proposal.

Site visit first and proposal second; otherwise ,don't fool yourself…you're just submitting a "Bid."

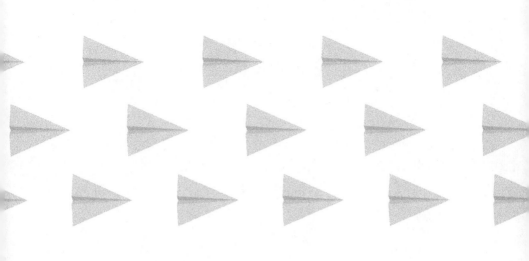

SECTION 4

WINNING

"Every sale has five basic obstacles: no need, no money, no hurry, no desire, no trust."[50] *– Zig Ziglar*

[50] brainyquotes.com

CHAPTER 10

Closing and Negotiation

I do not care for the terms "closing" or "deal" or "moving to contract." And yet I will admit to, on occasion, having used two of those terms – "closing" and "deal." I like to think I did so sparingly and never in front of the customer. And as far as "moving to contract" goes, this sure sounds like classic corporate speak, to me – unemotional, detached and sterile. These same salespeople say "walk-ins" when talking about potential customers who show up without an appointment to review their facilities. They are also the same ones who like to say they will meet their appointments in the "closing room" (sounds ominous, or like a doctor going into the "OR") instead of in the reception area.

Of course, "closing" or "booking business" is the ultimate goal in sales. Just as there are many who keep trying to close too soon and too quickly, there are just as many who never close. The latter, as much as they will rationalize their behavior, are simply afraid and do not ask for the business. In both cases, neither has that clear sense of touch we have discussed. Because they have not established enough of a connection with the prospective buyer and have not evaluated where they really are on the court with the buyer throughout the process, they end up picking the wrong – or no – moment to close at all.

THE CLOSE

There is nothing dramatic about closing. It's nothing more than the natural conclusion of all that has gone before it. The end ("The Close") really starts at the very beginning. A successful close is determined by how much you concentrate your efforts on what's most important to your prospective customer, and how you most effectively demonstrate you are working on a win-win basis. No attempt to close should be made, of course, until you have established value in the customer's mind.

If you are a good salesperson, you made small trial closes all the way through the sales process as you moved from one step to the next. You would have listened and questioned, discovered needs and wants, and then presented back a proposal that addresses those very needs and wants. You would have then secured verbal confirmation that, yes, your proposal addressed each of that particular customer's needs and wants, and to his satisfaction. If you had correctly uncovered all critical information, you would actually see your customer selling himself on your product/service.

By contrast, inexperienced and ineffective salespeople are so eager to close their sales that they attempt to do so in a very haphazard way. This usually does not work. It comes across to the prospect as inexperience, incompetence or both, causing him to think: "Why should I take a chance on you?" Remember the "Five Whys"? So important. This is counterintuitive to what some salespeople believe. Based on what many salespeople do (as evidenced by the proposals we reviewed in Chapter 9), I can only think their actions are indicative of their beliefs. It is, however, ultimately never about products or features; it's about needs and how you can help achieve your prospect's goals. If you are looking to close more business, then you need to be constantly asking yourself:

> Am I "totally" locking in on this customer's objectives/needs?

Buying Signals

Whereas the term "closing" sounds like something that is done to or inflicted on the customer, "buying" sounds like something that emanates from the customer. One pushes against, the other pulls toward. The latter is the preferred and better avenue to success.

So, what are buying signals? They are both visual and behavioral. There can be an auditory component, too. The willingness to talk with me is already a buying signal. A facial expression and tone that reflects openness and a cooperative nature are signals, as well. A willingness to return calls, give straightforward and honest answers to my questions – these are further indicators. Actions and questions indicating implied consent are classic buying signals. When someone asks me a lot of questions, this, too, is a buying signal. When a prospective customer suddenly slows down the pace of the conversation, or suddenly speeds up, both can be buying signals, when viewed in context with the prospect's overall behavior. The same indicators as outlined in Chapter 8 – non-verbal communication – apply here, whether you are attempting to close in person or over the telephone.

Non-Buying Signals

Generally, when someone looks at his watch several times, nods a little too quickly, shifts his eyes side to side, frequently shuffles papers, sits across from you with arms crossed, starts referring to his next appointment, or starts pushing money as an issue a little too quickly – these are all non-buying signals. Tentative answers, non-answers, iffy answers, and a vague sense you are not connecting – same thing. Of course, taken individually, each may or may not be non-buying signals, that's why you need to evaluate the behavior within a larger context. Good salespeople look for the signals – both positive and negative – early in the process. Unfortunately, many salespeople don't look for the signals at all, and actually avoid or block out non-buying signals because they are on autopilot. When you get yourself enmeshed in talk about features, you can very easily lose track of any signal (good or bad) a prospective customer is sending.

In tandem with buying signals are asking buying questions. In other words, trial closes. The terms are interchangeable. The chief benefit of trial closes is that it keeps you – and the potential buyer – on track.

Some salespeople hardly ever ask buying questions though, because – you guessed it – they are afraid to. When I would talk with a salesperson about his or her conversations with various prospects I often got a lot of, "Well, I didn't ask them that...." or "They didn't say." And that said to me: Reactive, passive, not engaged and not hungry enough.

There are innumerable questions you can pose to your prospective customers – some during your first meeting, others, as noted, after they receive your proposal. As to when exactly you ask these questions, it all comes down to your sense of touch. How quickly or slowly the customer is moving through the sales process with you will determine when and where you pose these questions. Here are some buying questions that could generally be asked while you are meeting with a prospective customer and/or while touring your facility:

- What's your thinking on this?
- Are you with me so far?
- Does that all make sense to you?
- What would an ideal outcome be for you?
- Am I on the right track?
- Does that sound better than the way you have been doing it?
- Does it sound to you like we are getting to a solution to your problem?
- What questions do you have at this point?
- Is there anything I may have gone over too quickly?
- Is there something I should expand upon for you?
- Do you feel comfortable so far with what I have presented to you?

These are very simple, very direct questions framed and presented by you to elicit:

FEEDBACK

Besides keeping you on track, this more specific kind of feedback helps significantly in directing your next remarks. It might also uncover some unsuspected needs and – more importantly – unsuspected reservations the potential buyer has. You will find out what has not been said.

By testing the waters throughout the entire sales process, you can help ensure that when you do close the sale, you are closing on very solid ground. Notice too, all the questions focus on the customer's perception of value and problems. Untrained salespeople who quote their prices first (before the prospect fully understands the value being offered) are now left to deal with closing resistance.

I have often seen salespeople – after meeting with a prospective customer – who really don't know what happened, what was accomplished (nor, for that matter, what they were trying to accomplish) and most importantly, why or why not. You hear a lot of: "We had a pretty good meeting; we had a great conversation." Or: "I think I might get the event; I think they like me; I think they were really impressed." You need to confirm it. You need to confirm what they liked about you, why, and is what they liked enough to turn this prospect into a customer. And does "like" translate to "trust"? Exactly what were they impressed by? You need to ask these questions and, if need be, other uncomfortable questions, to get true confirmation.

What do you do about people pleasers? These individuals don't want to hurt your feelings, so they tell you what you want to hear and never quite decide. You have to learn to spot the behavior and then you need to change it up...and do the unexpected. Just say "All right, we agree. Where do we go from here?"

There will certainly be occasions when you will meet with a prospective customer, conduct a site visit and close the sale – all in one meeting. And there are just as many, if not more, occasions where you will submit a formal proposal after the site visit. In these instances, it is imperative to place a follow-up call, especially when there are several people involved in the decision-making process. This call is the true start of the closing and negotiation.

YOUR CLOSING CALL

It's pretty simple: In your proposal cover letter you said you would be calling, so you do. Based on what you have outlined in your proposal cover letter, you now have an excellent opportunity to pose a few (buying and closing) questions and listen very carefully to the responses. These questions might include:

- Have you had a chance to review our proposal? (do not say "my" proposal; "my" implies it's personal, and most people don't like to hurt anyone's feelings directly).
- How do you feel about our proposal?
- Are there any areas in our proposal where you need further clarification?
- Do you think our proposal will eliminate or reduce the problem issues we spoke about?
- How do we look from your vantage point?
- Does our proposal make sense to you?
- It appears you have a number of problems with your current venue. I believe we have the solutions to those problems. What do you think?
- Have I (now you can refer to you) left anything out?
- Is there anything else you need from me?
- Do you feel comfortable with what I have presented?
- Where do we go from here?

All of these questions are designed to bring you closer to signing a contract. Based on the answers, you will know if you need to explain something further or if you are all in agreement. If you have done your homework well, conducted a great site visit, asked lots of detailed questions and established rapport with the potential customer, odds are when they receive your proposal, it is going to pretty much reflect your discussion. If all agree, you will be moving naturally and logically to the buying stage. In most cases, the answer will be: "Thank you for sending me such a detailed proposal. It covers everything we discussed and more. I will review this with everyone tomorrow and should have it back to you by Thursday."

Stepping In

As is often the case, however, it doesn't go quite that smoothly. You might get a rather wishy-washy answer or no answer at all. Or, all of a sudden, you learn that the committee or the board will not meet on this for two weeks or so. What do you do? Average salespeople all of a sudden become very tentative at this critical juncture. You hear a lot of: "Okay, I see," and "When should I get back with you?" Real closers, though, experience an adrenaline rush at this point, because they know they are at a critical point in the sale. We said that in the early stages of a sale (soliciting/ prospecting and first meeting), our aim is to purposely slow down the conversation. In the latter stages (closing/negotiation phases) the aim is just the opposite. Average salespeople, by the way, ask very few of the closing questions I have outlined above. Whatever questions they do ask are usually not very direct nor proactive. And more to the point, their questions are not stated confidently. What do you think is being communicated non-verbally? Fearful salespeople say they don't want to speed things up because they don't want to put too much pressure on the customer; they don't want to "scare him off." And so...the illusion of selling plays on.

So, what do the top closers do? They step in. They actually do considerably more than that. As we say in tennis, they "move up to net," to put a little bit more pressure on their opponent. In sales you do this by the pace and tone of the conversation. You are – very politely – applying more pressure and the questions are coming a little bit faster. Yes, good salespeople keep going on offense; they step in more and...

Probe Deeper...Going in for the Kill

Some examples:

- I just want to be absolutely certain, does our proposal address all the issues/needs you articulated to me?
- Do you personally feel comfortable enough (not the committee or the board) and trust in my recommendations enough to move forward?

- Is there something I am missing?
- Is there something that has held you back in the past from going with us that I should be aware of?
- Under what circumstances could you see moving forward on this?
- If I can find a way to meet your needs for _____ , and it makes good business sense for both of us, would you be more inclined to strongly consider our venue for your fall conference?
- Am I making any progress today in terms of convincing you to use our venue?
- How do we look in comparison to our competition?
- What do you think has to happen for you to go with us?
- Not to assume but, if everything we have discussed here makes sense to you, how soon would you like to confirm?
- What is your biggest obstacle to moving forward on this (or getting this done)?
- If you alone (not your boss) had to make the decision today, would you go with us?
- On a scale of 1 to 10, where are you?
- What do we have to do to get you to a 10?

All of your questions are designed to get to the truth, but this second group – the more probing questions – are intended to put a little more direct buying pressure on the prospect. The idea here is to encourage the person you are speaking with to respond, "Yes, if…." and not, "No, because….". You need to know: What are we really dealing with? What is the key issue we need to address to move this from "no" to "yes"? And you have to assume you are at "no" until you flush out the answers to these questions.

There are certainly enormous advantages to having this conversation face to face. And, for a select few accounts, this is probably the best way to get to the truth. In most cases, though, this conversation will be by telephone, and this can be even more effective. The telephone offers a buffer between both parties, while it is, at the same time, a very personal way to move things forward. Face to face, the customer might be hesitant to say, directly, what the issue is. He knows you have worked hard to gain his business. He is hesitant to hurt your feelings. That's why the more indirect use of a telephone at this point in the sale can be much more effective at getting to the real issues.

The Customer Can Say No??

Ultimately, as a salesperson, you have to convey the message that it is okay for the potential customer to say no. Why? You have to show you can accept not having their business today, to give you a chance of ever having their business tomorrow. You can say, for example: "Look, we (not I) certainly want to and would welcome the opportunity to work with you on this event. But, if we are not going to have that opportunity, it is equally important we know why not. Where have we gone wrong?" Then shut up and listen for the answer. Remember though, only a confident salesperson who has established a relationship of trust and candor with the customer can ask any of these questions and not alienate the prospect. Of course, your question (which is, in essence, forcing a decision) might lead to the prospect saying you/your venue has been eliminated altogether and why. This won't be the answer you want to hear, but it's very important, nonetheless. You will then need to focus on the "why" portion of his response. On the other hand, the more likely response will be: "No definite decision has been made yet "but…." Whatever they say after "but" is the basis of the final stage of the sale – namely, the negotiation.

Note: In this case, I would still probe a bit, just to further clarify the prospect's position and to determine what the negotiation will be about. I also might summarize aloud what the issues are and then ask, "Is there anything else I should be aware of," or say, "Would that be a correct summary of the issues as you see it?" I would then conclude by thanking him for being so candid with me. I would let him know I will review this new information and get back to him before the committee meets/ makes a final decision.

See how effective and imperative it is to have this direct telephone conversation with the prospect at this critical juncture? Could you have done this by email and had a result that moves things forward? It's highly unlikely. With electronic communication, you can hide and, more importantly, the potential customer can hide. You can get basic surface-level responses, but you cannot get at the root cause of any delay. It actually contributes to backward movement. If the prospect has four proposals and you are the only provider who calls directly to follow up, you are well ahead of the pack. The prospect has no other option but to have a direct personal conversation with you, because you stepped in and stepped up the pace of the game.

The Famous "What Ifs"

What if... the prospective customer says he is not ready to make a decision? We can ask what he would need to know before he would feel ready to take action. Then we have to make sure we meet those stated needs. A variation on this is when the customer says, "I don't know." We can immediately respond with "Well, what would you say if you did know?" You would be amazed at the responses you get.

What if... the potential customer says: "Well, we are looking at several venues/a number of proposals." The inexperienced salesperson will say, "When will you be making a final decision?" The strong salesperson will say "Based on everything we have discussed up until now, is there any reason you would not go with us?" If the potential customer says no, then simply ask them: "If you were me, what would you do to keep the momentum moving in our direction?" They will tell you.

What if... you are dealing with an argumentative/very negative hard liner? Surprise him. Be as agreeable as possible. If he continues to criticize, let him talk and talk (appeal to his ego). Listen carefully, and latch onto whatever common ground you can determine.

What if... he says, "We're considering other options." You can respond, "I certainly can understand the importance of making the right decision. As you continue the evaluation process, what is the specific criteria you are looking to address?" Another response would be to say, "You mentioned other options, which tells me I failed to address something that must be important to you. Can you tell me what that is?"

*What if...*he says he has to talk it over with someone. My response would be, "Can I interpret that as a definite sign of interest?" Or a stronger approach: "When you do talk it over will you be recommending us?'

*What if...*he says: "I will never pay that price." When someone makes this kind of dramatic, over the top kind of remark –the best advice is to simply ignore it. Don't ask for clarification, because usually this is not a true ultimatum. This is a complaint, not a true objection. If he keeps saying it over and over again, then you probably have no other choice but to ask him to give you specifics as to his price concerns.

What if... he says the rather vague, "Yes, we do have some concerns about booking this event with you." Or, just as bad, but a bit more subtle, the potential customer hesitates and won't commit at all. What's going on? You need to pause and then ask that wonderfully versatile question we talked about in Chapter 2: "Why and where have I missed the mark?" It gives him a chance to explain himself and it gives you a chance to change his mind.

Above all, you don't want to be confrontational, but you do want to be candid, forthright and transparent. You also need to resist that all-too-human urge to jump in and try to fix it, by coming back with an immediate response. It will do absolutely nothing for you at this important moment. To stay in the game, you need to settle down and relax. Resist the natural urge to be defensive and listen more carefully than ever before. Show that you are really taking it all in, absorbing everything he is saying. You will hear just about all the vital information you need to move forward, as long as you simply listen and don't respond immediately.

Why Would They Say That?

When the potential customer says, "Yes, we do have some concerns," (or they hesitate/remain silent), usually one of four dynamics are in play:

1. The potential customer doesn't fully understand the solution you are presenting.

2. You have not fully understood some and/or all aspects of the problem.
3. You lost his attention. He was distracted.
4. He doesn't trust you.

Here's where you have to use a certain amount of diplomacy. In the case of scenario 1. you might say, "Have I convinced you that you will not encounter the same quality/service problems with us that you have experienced with XXX venue?" If yes, then continue closing. If no, say, "Where have I missed the target?" You need to take responsibility for any miscommunication, whether correct or not.

The first three scenarios are very easy to address. Just go back and, through questioning, establish and reconfirm a few items. It might be as simple as repeating what you already told him with some slight clarification on one or two specific points. But what about scenario 4.? What if he doesn't trust you?

THE NUMBER ONE REASON: LACK OF TRUST

The number one reason people do not buy is "Uncertainty." Translation: "Lack of trust." It's your job to be aware of and sensitive to this, and to uncover in full what, exactly, the uncertainty is. This is exactly the point where so many flinch, retreat and fail to address the issue head on. This is, however, exactly the moment you must step up and take ownership of the game. With confidence, empathy and honesty. You have to address the issue.

Andre Agassi was one of the best returners of serve in tennis, because he stepped in and took the ball early, no matter who his opponent was. The same is true with successful salespeople. They step in and engage, versus stepping back and reacting or, worse, acting as if nothing is wrong. Ineffective salespeople revert back to "think, wish, hope" – they think the less said the better. With many salespeople, this avoidance of confrontation (no matter how subtle) means they are choking.

Most people, however, are not going to flat out tell you they don't trust you. But by process of elimination and a good sense of feel you can figure it out. This is what I would say:

"I feel I am offering you some very legitimate and realistic solutions to the issues you presented. However, being very candid and at the risk of perhaps being a little too direct (smile when you say this), I don't think you trust me, in the sense I suspect you are probably thinking to yourself, 'I'm just not sure he can or will deliver on everything he has said. Can you suggest any ways that I could change that perception and gain your trust?" And then you continue looking at him but, most important, you shut up and wait for a response.

Typically, people will respond that they just need time, or they need to think about it. The first thing I have to decide then is: Is this prospect worth the continued investment of my time? For discussion purposes, I am assuming the answer is yes. Let him or her know then you would like to stay in touch but will not make a pest of yourself. Based on this strategy, you are starting to move closer to a sale. This prospect just said, "No, not now." You, however, have added the unspoken part: "Yes, but maybe later. "Just like in tennis, keep it moving. If you stand still, you lose.

THINK BIG PICTURE

In the event of the above scenario, I would initially send this prospect a short note attaching a testimonial letter from a happy customer you worked with whose needs/concerns and event were similar to those of your prospect. If the testimonial letter is from a similar organization, even better. Based on the customer's time horizon, I would continue to follow up every month or so over a three- to six-month period with a very short note. On the second follow-up, I would enclose a testimonial letter from a client I have worked with for 10 years. State that you believe this clearly shows they trust you, because you have met their needs for all this time. Add that you hope he will see this as evidence you would do the same for his organization. On the third follow-up I would say, "What about talking directly to some of our customers? I have asked a few if they would be willing to take your call and give candid feedback on their experience with our company. Would you be willing to call one or two of these customers? I have attached a list with their names, companies and contact information."

Throughout all this correspondence, it is critically important that you remain professional, friendly, confident and non-threatening. Don't hound them. To maintain a positive attitude, remind yourself that you have clearly and honestly established that the potential customer needs or wants exactly what you are selling, and they have shown some real interest in buying from you. If that is not the case, you may very well be perceived as a pest at a minimum or, worse, a stalker.

My last follow-up would be an extremely short note. I might very well include a small box of cookies from our award-winning pastry chef. My note would run along the lines of saying, "I hope you have found my notes to be helpful, informative and effective. I would like you to have these cookies as a thank you for all the consideration you have already given me these last three to six months." I would then wrap it up by saying, "I will call you in a few days to see if the information I have been sending you has been helpful, and if you are ready to take the next step of actually doing business together."

Work Your Plan

By now, it should be clear how important it is to present yourself as a skilled professional who knows your product/services. You want the prospect to know you expect him or her to buy from you because you offer the very best value package. At the same time, you need to present yourself as open and non-threatening. If the potential customer does not like your location or the image of your facility, you need them to tell you that. You need to encourage them to be as frank with you as possible. A planned presentation is a huge advantage in this regard. Armed with a plan, I have a well-thought-out road map to success. Most importantly, it frees me up to observe all of those non-verbal customer responses – tone, inflection, pace, facial expressions and body language. With a written, well-practiced plan as my platform, I am able to…

- ...perfect my actual presentation, while allowing for slight adjustments, based upon my direct interaction with each customer.
- ... inject variation in rhythm and timing, pacing and emotion.
- ...incorporate natural inflection points.
- ...keep my entire focus on them, not me.

> Tennis players watch film footage of their upcoming opponents to get a better sense of how they will execute against a particular player in the coming week. A written plan is the salesperson's equivalent of this exercise. It frees you up to play the game - to step in and not back up.

NEGOTIATION

Learning to negotiate is one of the most important and also one of the most difficult parts of selling. Why? The fact is, many salespeople do not like to negotiate. That might seem surprising and even contradictory. After all, salespeople are always negotiating, right? On the surface it can appear that way ("the all motion is progress" swirl), but, in fact, when you honestly look at it, a lot of salespeople are "negotiated by" not "negotiating with" potential customers.

The two most important things I can tell you about negotiation are: Price is rarely the determining factor we can all-too-often be led to believe it is – or believe ourselves. And second: Negotiation is all about finding solutions. Of course, we negotiate on all sorts of levels and in all sorts of situations every day of our lives. As applied to selling though, many salespeople don't like conflict, which is inherent in negotiation; it makes them feel uncomfortable, even fearful. Still others, having negotiated, often walk away with that gnawing feeling that the other person got the better of the deal. And a few simply will do almost anything to avoid actually having to sit down and negotiate with someone about anything. These are huge mistakes. The object of negotiation is not to sneak something by the buyer, nor is it to give away the store. In short:

The purpose of negotiation is to develop a "mutually beneficial agreement," which provides value to both sides. To be very specific about it...

> ...reaching an agreement is not the purpose. A good negotiation results in an agreement that makes you better off than you would have been otherwise.

Many salespeople worry so much about price. I tell them not to worry too much about negotiating with price-sensitive customers, because they are more apt to up and leave you without a second thought anyway. These people are easy to win by just cutting your prices, but that means they will also be very easy to lose to some other "also ran" down the road. The same applies to raising prices. Even if you lose a few customers, it's better than underselling yourself to "keep the business" or to "preserve market share."

It sounds so obvious but think back. There are probably a few times in all our careers where we voluntarily said yes to an offer that made us worse off. The other person needs to know what we need, as well. It is important to not only tell them what you need but also why. Implicit in this is that the true spirit of a positive negotiation is to be fair and reasonable to both parties. It is to always be working on the basis of a two-way street.

Unfortunately, too many salespeople don't accept this very basic and simple truth about customers and price. They telegraph "desperation" to their potential customers, by their choice of words, tone and inflection, but mostly by their body language and facial expressions. Some will call this "hunger to close," but I don't buy it. Three core principles apply when we talk about negotiation:

1. Nobody wants to pay more than they "have to" for anything.
2. People will pay more when they feel they are getting more for their money.
3. Price is rarely the determining factor we all so often allow ourselves to falsely believe it is.

If you believe price rules, you will always be at a severe disadvantage in the negotiating phase, and the potential customer will sense it immediately. Until you accept these core principles of negotiation, you will always be a truly hopeless underdog in the sales game.

Backing Up…Falling Down

In the everyday real world of sales, you submit a formal proposal and, a few days later, make your follow up call. What if the response is, "Thank you for your proposal, but you are really much more expensive than everyone else we met with." What now? Do you hesitate? Do you freeze? Many do. Or, they start to sputter and talk very quickly. How many times have you heard: "Oh, let me get back to you; let me review the price"; or "We can do better; there is room for negotiation"; or, the worst possible: "Let me check with my director." These are all dead giveaways that you are nervous and lack confidence – both in yourself and your product/service. This fear and intimidation sets in motion a train of self-defeating comments and non-verbal cues – none of which are positive or helpful in the situation.

Now, many will say, "I never make comments like…" the ones I have outlined. I agree, many don't. Instead what many do – *their actions* – are what betray them. Haven't you seen a salesperson:

- "Fade" from one price to a lower number with no negotiation at all. (I have never understood this one, yet it happens all the time).
- "Saving Face." A flimsy rationale is offered – some minor detail in the proposal – to justify lowering the price. This "Saving Face" scenario is so embarrassing.
- Simply drop the price, without even attempting to counter, thus inviting even more negotiation.
- Refuse to negotiate, saying this is the price and that's that. This tends to be the response of extremely inexperienced salespeople who work in very basic facilities.

None of these approaches are very good or effective in either the short- or the long-term. They are, however, more the norm than the exception in our industry. I have seen contracts with 10 to 15 concessions. I have even seen contracts with extremely discounted pricing to begin with, further compounded by an additional 23 concessions. That's not a negotiation; that's a shellacking!

When you employ any of these negotiating strategies, your words and actions breathe new life into the prospect's price objection and tell the buyer you are backing up. When someone says, "Let me check with my director," or the more generic, "...check with my team," they have totally negated their own power. The key here is most buyers do not trust most sellers, especially when it comes to price. That's because we have trained them that way. Many customers are conditioned to complain about the first price you give them. Countless times, their experience has shown them that most sellers will almost immediately lower their price when confronted with any price objection. At the same time, many salespeople work off the assumption they have to compromise. But you don't want to be like most salespeople, so what will you do when they say your prices are too high?

> Politely decline the invitation to be intimidated and accept the invitation to explain why your prices best serve the needs of this particular customer for this particular event.

I know, it sounds ridiculously easy, but just tell them why they should be buying from you even though your price is higher. I should preface this by saying you should always expect potential customers to raise a price objection. No need to be surprised. And when they do, all you have to do is go back to the beginning.

Go Back to Square One...To the Very Beginning

Start asking more questions. Go back to all those notes you took in the very beginning, which pointed you toward their buying signals:

- **Value:** What is important to them? What will make the event a success as far as they are concerned? What are their real needs and wants?
- **Pain:** What were the problems and the worries in the past?
- **Better Way:** What are some of the better ways you have offered to reduce or eliminate pain? What have you offered that differentiates you from your competition?
- **The Smile Question:** and his specific answer to that question. (See Chapter 8).

Of course – most important – listen to what your potential customer says about your pricing and verify exactly what is included and not included in the competition's proposal (and secure the name of the competitor if you do not already have it). Usually, there will be differences (for example, your price package includes a full continental breakfast and the competition is offering an extremely modified coffee break, or the portion size could be smaller, or you offer four bottles of wine with dinner and the competition offers only two, etc.) and the competing facility in all probability has purposely used vague language and much less detailed notes in their proposal. You can then confidently and calmly say one of the following:

- "Yes, we are a little more expensive than X. Let me tell you exactly why."
- "Yes, we are more expensive There is a saying and it does tend to be true: You usually pretty much get what you pay for in this world. In our case, here's how we...."
- "Yes, we are one of the higher priced venues in the city. Not the most expensive, but still on the higher side, nonetheless.

Our customers use us knowing they have absolutely nothing to worry about. Let me explain, specifically, what I mean by that."

You then go right back and key into the four points outlined above, along with any discrepancies you have picked up on in the competition's proposal. It is imperative that your body language, tone and inflection all convey confidence, strength, openness, empathy and knowledge. And that you are not the least bit surprised or taken aback by the prospect's remarks.

BEFORE YOU GO THERE

Before you even set foot into a negotiation, you'll want to review your proposal one more time and ask yourself: "How do I think my proposal stacks-up versus the competition? What do I think is the difference and is it worth it to the customer?" Based on honest answers to these questions (which could have changed from your original meeting), you will be in a much better negotiating posture as you move forward.

Note: Of even more importance, you have to know what you will do if you do not reach an agreement with this prospective customer. It gives you a tremendous psychological advantage going in, because you already know you don't have to make this sale. It gives you an edge, relaxes you and non-verbally communicates that you are stepping in and not desperate.

Any good and fair negotiation should be negotiated in this order:

1. VALUE

You are getting more for your money with our proposal. Promote the difference between your product and services and those of your rivals. Revisit all the values. Go back to what the potential customer said is important to them and what would make the event a success for them. Whatever that "more" is, it must be directly tied to the customer's "stated" needs and wants. In essence, go back to all those questions you asked (qualifying) in the very beginning, reminding the prospect of his own stated needs and wants.

2. Pain

You go back and review how your proposal greatly alleviates or eliminates the pain altogether. Now it's time to press your points:

- **Put the risks on the table** – the risks you uncovered when you first inquired about their prior experience(s).
- **Remind them** that the last time they did this event they got what they paid for (and it was not good!)
- **Explain** that your price may be higher, but it includes insurance against whatever problem they had happening again.
- **Remind them** your price is really the lowest, most cost-effective way of getting what they really want.

As noted earlier, Andre Agassi (and today Novak Djokovic) are the best returners of serve. Andre's focus was riveted on that tennis ball, and he "anticipated" ever so slightly better than everyone else where that serve would land. He was then able to step in to return the ball a little bit quicker and earlier than his opponent expected. The same analogy applies with putting risk on the table early, especially when entering the closing/negotiation phase. While your natural tendency may be to be surprised, go on the defensive and instinctively step back, you should actually go on offense. I have outlined below two examples of what I call "aggressive negotiation," with respect to discussing risk. In the first case, there were immediate results. In the second, the results were not so immediate but were certainly long lasting.

"Risk Discussion" Example 1: I had worked with a particular organization for about 20 years. The executive director of this organization had recently retired. Shortly after meeting the new executive director,

I realized this individual was "on a mission." He had looked at three other venues for his association's event, had ruled out two, but was seriously considering the third. Nonetheless, he wanted to see what our venue had to offer. I went through my plan – value/pain, cost and price – to no avail. He didn't care, and said his attendees wouldn't care, about our "creative desserts," upgraded plate presentations and our provision of more service personnel. Even though for all these years, these had been key requirements. I was now told his guests were more interested in watching the entertainment, drinking wine and networking. This executive director kept beating the drum: Lower pricing!

I put together a second written proposal outlining the clear advantages we offered, plus I revised the menu using less expensive/cost-effective appetizers and desserts and readjusted the price point accordingly. When I called to see what he thought, again I was greeted with "Price, Price and – you guessed it – Price! Then he went one step too far, telling me he had spoken with Z Organization, which we had worked with for many years, saying Z had decided to go with this same competitor (he was strongly considering) for their event. He said the Z group was extremely happy with the venue.

Well, I said (here's where that knowledge habit and the concept of stepping in come into play) if Z Organization was so happy with the XXX venue, then why are they rebooked with us for next year? The executive director was speechless. Though the person did start to recover and go on the attack again, I upped the ante (stepped in, took the ball early). I told him he had all the necessary information from us to make an informed and final decision. I suggested he go back and speak with Z Organization again, and I told him we would need a final answer in 48 hours. End of conversation. Silence ensued for 48 hours and then...he booked with us.

"Risk Discussion" Example 2: I worked with an association that had an annual dinner for 1,000 people every spring. One year I got a big surprise: The association's new leadership said they would be going to the XXX Venue for the following year due to much lower pricing, etc. It was too late in the game to really do anything, however, I did make it a point to say: "I know the venue very well and I strongly believe they lack the ability to properly execute the choice of entrées we do (choice of entrees for 1,000 people – not easy), no matter what they say to the contrary. What good is it to have a lower price if they cannot execute the service of the meal?" This was all based on my extensive knowledge of the other facility's operational procedures and capabilities. I indicated that, from an operational standpoint, all pointed to a very serious if not impossible challenge for the venue selected. I even put this in writing to them after our conversation, mostly because I was so sure of my prediction. It was to no avail; they had made up their minds.

The following spring, I purposely attended the association's annual golf outing, held a few days after the annual dinner. I was greeted with several comments about what a disaster the annual dinner had been. Over 200 people left without getting served their dinner! They signed a contract with us for next year's dinner very shortly thereafter and resumed being one of our long-standing accounts.

This is winning the long game, by establishing trust and integrity. This is what ultimately secured the sale. If I had not bothered to state my case at the time so directly and forcefully, the following year I would be just another venue in the mix. By stepping in, I not only led the pack the following year, I had already won by the end of that year's disastrous event! Attending the golf outing was yet a further example of stepping up and stepping in with confidence. It is aggressive and direct. Many do not do it, but it works. The one who puts risk on the table first usually benefits the most. You need to stay focused, remind them of the pain, remind them of the price of failure.

The morale of both stories: Ask assertive closing questions, make assertive closing statements; otherwise you will be a prisoner of "think, wish, hope."

3. Cost

If you cannot reach enough of an agreement on value and pain points, then you will probably have to move on to cost. You bring the price down by bringing down the costs – in other words, by offering less. You change an upgraded appetizer to a simpler dish, changing the entrée or portion size. You offer name brands vs. top shelf brand liquors on the bar and/ or different wines with dinner. The same type of revisions would apply with breakfasts, luncheons and coffee breaks. Using the same meeting room set up for an afternoon meeting as was used in the morning for another meeting can partially offset some of the labor costs and therefore, reduce the rental costs. The customer will get the lower price they want, and you get the solid profit you want. Of course, there has to be a certain give-and-take in the process. If you sense you are dealing with a "Price Hound," not a "Price Negotiator," you may have to just state your position and be ready to walk away, though this is very unlikely at this stage of the game if you have a fully qualified, legitimate prospect.

4.Price

Now, earlier I said the best salespeople anticipate price objections and start looking early in the game for leverage points to raise value, not lower pricing. That still applies, and yet are there times when it is really the best business decision to secure volume based on lower profit? Although it seems contradictory, the answer is yes...*occasionally*. There are a few extraordinary events (for example, those involving major celebrities with major media coverage and/or highly prestigious events), where significantly reduced pricing could be offered, in exchange for publicity and notoriety for your venue. This is, however, definitely the exception. Regardless, keep in mind that whenever you make a sale based on price, it reflects weakness and vulnerability – not strength – even under the best of circumstances.

Note: When entering into a negotiation on price: You first need to confirm price is, in fact, the issue by saying, "If we set price aside for a moment, are you comfortable enough with the product/services you want and the organizational support you need to buy from us?"

If the prospects response is "No" or "Maybe," then price is not the only issue. You will first need to determine what concerns the buyer and address those objections. Negotiating price is meaningless if a customer does not want to buy what you are selling to begin with. A very simple formula to counter this is as follows:

Closing Out the Point:

1. **Blunt:** "I hear exactly what you are saying. I can tell price is important to you as it should be. It is always an important consideration, particularly for an event of this size and scope."
2. **Question:** "It would be helpful if you could tell me a little more about why you think our prices are too high. Why you think we should discount this 20%?"
3. **One More Thing:** "Are there any other concerns I should be aware of?" If the customer says no, then you move on.
4. **Address:** "If I could address your concerns as to price and to our mutual satisfaction, would we be able to move forward?" If the potential customer hesitates, move to the next step.
5. **Something Else:** "Obviously something else is holding you back. Can we discuss this?"
6. **The List:** The person rattles off a list of five or six items they say are cause for concern. Usually one or two items need to be addressed immediately; often, you have addressed one or two of the issues before and you just need to remind them and review again. You may also determine that one or two other items can be addressed later after the major decision has been made. You may even decide that an item is really so trivial there is no need to respond (unless the prospect brings it up again).
7. **Respond:** "I know what you are saying (feeling); I would probably have felt the same way. What I have found though is…." Then provide them with a compelling story about a real customer you have worked with and how that situation turned out so successfully. This response is more commonly referred to as the "Feel, Felt, Found" rebuttal.
8. **Resolve:** The situation is only resolved after you have confirmed that it is with the potential customer. Get that, "Yes, I see your point" commitment back.

You can apply this format with all objections. Simply stated, a good part of your job is to uncover the reasons behind what the prospective customer perceives to be a risk or objection, let him express it, show that you understand it, and then eliminate it.

Now, back to our discussion of providing significantly discounted pricing. When, in the unusual situation of having to sell price (I realize this appears to run counter to what I have been preaching, that control needs to remain in your hands), make sure you convey that price is not solely your (the salesperson's) decision. It must be presented as a decision reached by upper management (general manager) after extensive consultation with you. In this situation, even though you are a conduit in this conversation, you are a very important and essential conduit who is speaking on behalf of the potential customer's needs. You state that in this very unusual one-time situation, we have decided to lower our price for these specific reasons, and then enumerate them. Presented correctly, the price itself is not your sole decision, and you imply or state that the offer is good for a reasonably short period of time. The potential customer starts to think this is a take-it-or-leave-it situation and he'd better start taking while the taking is good. When presented correctly, the control remains where it should be – firmly in your hands. To my point, let's review the following example:

"Price Discussion" Example

An organization hosts a large number of events throughout the year. You would certainly like to secure a healthy percentage of their business and, based on your meeting/discussion with them, you have determined there are several issues with the facility they are currently using. At the same time, they do not fully believe in the value you are offering. You feel strongly if they host just one function with you, they will come to see the clear value and upgrades your venue is offering. In other words, once they experience it for themselves, you will have proven your value, and the potential customer will sign up for more events with you at your regular pricing. In this situation, there is nothing wrong with saying, "Look, I think we can agree you have some issues with your current facility. I think we can also agree you see and, for the most part, believe, we have greater value to offer you and your guests. The stumbling block as I see it, though, is as much as you believe this, I still have not been able to quite convince you 100% as to the true value we offer. So, I would still ask you to give us a try and see for yourself the difference in value. I know in order to put forth this proposition, I cannot ask you to pay our regular pricing. Therefore, in this one instance, we will match the price point you are currently paying, in order to give you a strong enough reason (based on a very successful first event with us) to contract with us for 40% of your future events. I do want to be very clear, though, and make sure you fully understand that, after the first event, we intend to charge our higher pricing as outlined in our proposal. We would expect you would gladly pay these higher prices after a successful experience. How does that sound to you? Shall we move forward?" Then shut up and wait for a response. Don't forget: You need to get something significant for anything you give up. Otherwise, how can the buyer ever again trust you regarding price or anything else? What else are you going to drop on? Quality? Service? There is no recovery from this, because you have planted in the mind of the customer a seed of doubt.

Especially in a down economy, there will always be that temptation – and pressure – to negotiate down pricing. But remember, downturns and recoveries come and go. The best salespeople focus on where they want to be when the market recovers and the upturn inevitably happens. In short, when negotiating on price:

1. It has to be very specific and clearly articulated to the customer.
2. It has to be limited with conditions on each party.
3. You must absolutely get something in return.

In other words, "If I do this…you will do this." Quid pro quo. The significant something could be a two-year contract instead of one year. Or, it could be hosting another one of their conferences with you. Keep it very simple and you will keep your self-respect, as well as your customer's trust.

I employed this strategy with several organizations I worked with over the years. I secured one group's first event for $60,000. This led to a total of $500,000 in additional short-term business (booking within a 60- to 90-day window) from the same organization over the course of one year.

HANDLING THE STALL

When dealing with someone who appears to be stalling, you have to rely on your sense of touch. You know what you are going to say; what's more important is how you say it. Particularly at this juncture in the sales process, a potential customer can be very touchy. He reacts more to the sound of your voice and gestures than to the words themselves. This is where that "good sense of touch around the "greens" comes in. You absolutely have to keep it positive, almost playful – light, relaxed and friendly. This is all much easier to do if you have already established with yourself what you will do if, at the conclusion, you do not have an agreement. When a person is stalling ("I have to think it over"), here are a few useful follow ups:

- "Of course, what aspects do you feel require further thought?"
- "When you are ready to make a decision, what will be the things most important to you in making that decision?"
- "I'm sure you have a reason for wanting to think it over. May I ask what that reason is?
- "I understand your wanting to think this over. I would be interested, though, in knowing your thoughts as to the reasons for and against making this purchase now."
- Another approach would be to say, "I understand you want to wait. But I want to make sure we are prepared for you when you are ready. What can we do now to make sure all of our ducks are in a row?"
- Another tactic to employ when confronted with stalling is to break the rhythm. "It sounds like there is just no way we can make this work." After stating this, remain silent. Most people hate to feel they have failed, so this might get your prospect to re-engage in the sales process.

Such questions start the person thinking about what they will do when the time is right. Often, just shifting the discussion this way results in the "right" time coming about much sooner than you would think.

DEALING WITH A DIFFICULT NEGOTIATOR

- When a prospect asks for the impossible just say, "How do you suppose we do that?"and then remain silent. This actually encourages your prospect to solve the problem for both of you. It also forces them to take a really close look at your situation.

- When a prospective customer makes a demand or states a position, ask a question: "Exactly, why do you want that?" Based on the response you will be able to ask even more questions and gain more information that can lead you to negotiating a compromise or tradeoff.

- When offering options at the end of your comments say: "Of course, it is up to you." This encourages cooperation and helps diminish resistance.

- Summarize the prospective customer's feelings about the proposal presented as completely as possible. Your intention is to have them say, "Yes, that's right." The result of this is the prospect feels you have stated their position very honestly and truthfully and they feel you have empathy for their position. The combination helps in moving them forward to a workable solution for all.

- They say, "Your prices seem high." Your response: "That's an important consideration, (name). As I see it, your question is, does the additional value in our product more than offset the higher price? Would I be correct in saying that?"

- Repeating the last three words someone says is also very effective and is similar to the mirroring we discussed in Chapter 8. The customer will feel in sync with you and will probably fill the silence by revealing more information and/or improving his offer. If the prospect's terms are inflexible, he will simply repeat them back word for word. If he has some leeway, he will expand on his description of the terms, adding lots of extra words. He may even start to reveal an uncertain tone and/or suddenly lower the demand.

- When negotiating numbers, as often as possible, ask your prospect for a figure first, but be on guard for the tough negotiator who then throws out a low-ball number. These offers are attempts at anchoring your thinking and conversation to their number. So whether the number is high or low, you could end up agreeing to or accepting much less than you should. A great response to this tactic again is to say, "How would you suggest I do that?"

- When you have to contradict a difficult customer, be diplomatic: "Yes, I can see why it would appear that way at first glance, however...." or, "Yes, many people do have that impression. However, as a matter of fact...."

Note: Keep in mind, when neither side wants to back down, it's not going to be enough that your proposal is an excellent offer. How can you expect this person to say yes and still go back to his organization and say he won? Figure out a few "flexible" ways you can make it easier for him to say yes. In other words, help him save face.

Walking Away

Supposing you are in a situation where you don't want to negotiate your price, and/or you have made all the adjustments you are willing to make. Accept it. You are not going to win every sale. If you have put forth a fairly priced proposal, have been flexible and candid in discussing value, cost and price, and they are still leaning elsewhere, then you need to hold firm. With very little hesitation, say:

- "I would very much like to have your business. At the same time, I also understand and accept that you are not in a position at this time to move forward."

Or:

- "I am, of course, disappointed we will not have the opportunity to be of service to your company and to work with you on this event. I would like to stay in touch with you, however."

Or:

- "I have seen that sometimes I do not secure someone's business the first time we meet. It can often take a year or two, during which I get to know you and your needs a little bit better and you gain greater confidence in me. So, I would like to keep working with you. Perhaps there will be other events and/or smaller projects you have coming up in the course of the year. I hope we can work on these with you."

Note: Even though you are exiting the situation, you want to leave on good terms. This is also a perfect time to ask for any referrals.

Or:

- "We have put before you a very competitive proposal addressing all your needs. What you are asking for now could jeopardize the entire package."

You just might find after making this last statement they start coming back to the negotiation table. However, at this point, this cannot be your intent. The intent is to walk away, and on good terms.

The best salespeople are not afraid of losing a sale nor of being the first to walk away from a sale. They know the power of walking away. Again, you have to get to no quickly so you can move on to yes. Walk away so you can walk toward the prospects who are open to that conversation.

> Know what your bottom-line number is before
> you enter any negotiation and then stick with it.

WHAT DOES LOSING LOOK LIKE?

Unfortunately, there are a lot of terrible negotiators out there. Far from being the exception, it is more common to hear some of the following excuses/rationales:

- We generally need to cut our prices to get the business.
- It was a very competitive situation, so I needed to lower our price.
- I would rather close a deal at a lower margin than have no deal at all.
- The economy is tough, so we have to be realistic about our pricing.
- As a demonstration of our good faith, we will waive the room rental.
- Let me check on that.
- We don't want to lose the business, so what are we willing to do to keep it.

All these statements are giving away profit in order to close rather than negotiating objections. Think how often you hear, "Can we lower the menu price? Well, if we cannot do that can we lower the rental?" When I would ask why, I would be told "to show good faith." This is not good. You need to avoid salespeople like this. Whatever they have can be contagious.

Losing is usually marked by failing to differentiate you and your venue/services from your competitors. What seems to go along with this, as well, is failing to create a buying atmosphere.

What Does Winning Look Like?

The winners in sales:

- …offer and receive testimonial letters.
- … receive referrals.
- … offer their own experience.
- …raise values.
- …cut costs.
- … put "risk" on the table first.
- …provide relevant and provable facts, statistics and examples.
- …provide eye-catching pictures.
- …provide detailed and accurate diagrams and demonstrations.
- …have a walk-away…and stick with it.
- …never say no. Instead, they break the impasse with reason/or fair and reasonable tradeoffs.
- …have time on their side.
- …under promise and over deliver.

Here is an example of a successful and confident negotiation. For expediency sake, I have paraphrased the conversation:

Diane:

Jim, I hope you enjoyed this lovely summer. I reviewed the contract and would like for you to do better than $200 per person. Our rate was $190.00 last year. Can we do $194? I can take care of getting the signed letter to you between now and Monday. I'm in the office for another hour or so today and will be available tomorrow morning as well. I'll be in Chicago on business for a few days thereafter and back in the office on Mon. September 17th.

Jim:

Yes, Diane, I had a wonderful summer and I absolutely hate to see it go. Concerning our pricing, I purposely kept our increase as low as possible. We usually have increases of about 6-7% per year. In this case, our increase is 5% and was last year, as well. At the same time, in light of no rain all across the country, we know food costs will be rising rapidly and soon. There has been a lot of information in the news about this recently.

If your budget is restricted to $194 per person, I could make revisions to the menu to make the numbers work. I know you really do not want to do that, but there would be no other alternative.

Diane, looking at the bigger picture, I think we have always offered you outstanding value at a very competitive price point. And I think you are in agreement with me on this as well. However, with the projected increases in food costs, as well as annual labor increases – hard for us to control that – I think our total package is an excellent and very reasonable value.

Diane:

I expect outstanding value and am NOT willing to revise down the menu. I understand what you are saying. Thank you for keeping the increase at 5%. I appreciate it. This isn't a rep convention, it's the New York XXX Awards, an elegant black-tie gala honoring the best in media and I certainly want to maintain that. I'll sign the contract and send PDF via email.

I will have Deidre cut the deposit check. I'll sign today and have Nancy walk it over to your office either later today or Monday.

Good Negotiators

Good negotiators focus on the other person feeling satisfied; in other words, making sure their basic interests have been fulfilled. Good negotiators remember that a position is what a person says they want, but their basic interests are what they really need to get. Good salespeople also make clear to the customer what the salesperson's needs are and why he or she needs them. It can be easy to get caught up in the moment and think positions or complaints are objections. Think about it this way: Someone will say your price is too high, but similar to the weather, if it is too cold or too hot, do you really have any control over the weather?

Good negotiators, by definition, always have a large pipeline of leads/solicitations they are working on. It goes hand in hand – the more you have in the pipeline, the more confident you will be today in negotiating any deal. The less you have in the pipeline, the more anxious you will be.

Over Deliver

Referencing your success list in terms of negotiation – this is a huge weapon in your sales arsenal. If trust is your #1 weapon, then overdelivering is your second equally effective weapon, especially with repeat customers, and especially if you want to ensure repeat customers.

Always:

- **Answer your own phone as often as possible.** It says to new – but particularly existing – customers that you are always available. In today's world, it is a luxury not to get voicemail.

- **Anticipate needs.** "Will you need an early car service to the airport following tomorrow night's dinner? I would be glad to arrange it."

- **Be present.** Say you booked or re-booked a corporate meeting/luncheon for 400 guests. Be there at 7 a.m. to say, "Good Morning," and to ask if everything is going all right with the set up prior to the 9 a.m. start. You will probably startle your client, since many salespeople just don't do this anymore. Maybe he is having a small issue with the catering service manager that is working with him this morning and is hesitant to say anything. But he is more comfortable with you and knows you will understand. You then have the opportunity to step in and correct the situation right away; in other words, you can make it happen for him. If it wasn't clear before, at this point, your customers will know that you and your services are not a commodity.

- **Take the Experience Up a Level Every Year**

With repeat annuals ("Rock Stars"), being able to reference captain's reports highlighting any significant factors from last year's dinner (e.g., changes or, more important, any glitches, exact number of alternate meals, special requests or timing changes) all add to the experience. Offering refreshing and different menu choices each year also contributes to that effort.

Note: It is always a good idea to thoroughly review captain's reports as soon as possible the day after an event while things are still fresh in everybody's minds.

> If you over-deliver on a consistent basis, you very effectively set the stage for little to no resistance on annual price increases, you are more apt to get referrals, and you eliminate future competition before they can even get a hearing.

Please see Appendix B for "The Great Negotiator's Checklist."

Making it Happen

It is said Henry Kissinger believed that effectiveness at the bargaining table was dictated and dependent upon one's ability to simply overstate their initial demands. The idea is if you start higher, you leave yourself some negotiating room. The much more important reason, though, is that doing so leaves some room for the other person across the table to win something, too. You can call it the "saving face" approach, though I prefer to call it a "play nice in the sandbox" approach.

Throughout the entire sales process, you can be part of your own plan for success in a negotiation, or you can be part of the other party's. If you are anxious for a deal, by default you will be negotiating from the other side's playbook. It is, and must always be, your choice. The more negotiations you are involved in, the more confident you will become, and your performance will continue to grow. The same principle applies as with solicitation: The more you do it, the more contracts you will be signing.

A great negotiator must be able to hear and feel the rhythm and control the tempo of the discussion. You must intuitively know when it is advantageous to speed it up or slow it down or to stop the music completely. You also must sense when to be abrupt or abrasive, when to laugh, or when to walk away. Just like in tennis, you have to have a feel for what to do next, when to move in on a serve or when to play it back, when to hit top spin, when to hit a slice, when to lob it or go down the line, or when to surprise the other side with a drop shot. You have to know and have that feel for when to push it to the corners or quickly bring it up the middle.

The Cardinal Rules of Negotiation

As a reminder, outlined below, are your key survival tips:

 # 1: Always be willing to walk away. In advance of the negotiation, figure out how you will get by if the deal falls through. If you are depending on this sale, you lose your ability to negotiate, and the prospect senses it. In almost every case, the winner of a negotiation is the person best prepared for the possibility of the sale not happening at all. Figure out ahead of time what your other options are.

 # 2: The less trust you have developed with the customer the more prolonged and drawn out the negotiation will be, and usually it will be in a lop-sided manner favoring them. The more trust, the (much, much) less negotiation.

 # 3: No free gifts. Offer trade-offs for every concession.

 # 4: The person who has more time on his side has the biggest and best advantage in any negotiation.

#5: Customers have their own little "If I get this, I will buy" list. Our job is to find out what's on that list.

 # 6: Problems will always arise when someone wants to be right. Make sure it is not you.

And so, I will conclude this important segment on negotiation by repeating something I said in the beginning of this section on negotiation:

> Price is rarely the determining factor we all too often allow ourselves to believe it is. Don't forget it.

SECURING REFERRALS

Current customers will always be your best source for new customers. This assumes, of course, that their event is a total success, and their experience with you and everyone they come in contact with from your staff is pleasant and professional.

Just as you don't "make" a sale...you "earn" it; so, too, with referrals – you don't get them ...you earn them. One way to approach existing customers for referrals is to tell them they are your advertising, by saying, "If I treat you right with the best possible service and the best products, then I trust you will refer me. I am not going to ask you for a referral. I want to earn the right to be referable." Asking for a referral is one thing. Being referred is taking it to another level.

Another more aggressive approach would be to say, "I make my living working with people like yourself. Would you be willing to provide me with the names of three people you know who might be interested in having the same conversation?" The idea is to ask for three referrals, knowing you will probably only secure one, and will probably close on every third one.

Note: You have to be careful because, in essence, by asking for a referral, you are asking for a favor. Before asking, be sure your relationship with the customer will support this request.

The best referrals are rooted in trust. That's also why referrals tend to produce more profitable and more loyal customers. The most effective and powerful referrals actually happen without your doing anything. When one of your customers shares an unsolicited comment with someone else about what makes you such an effective salesperson, they are evangelizing for you by articulating your value. Your sources for referrals are not just limited to existing customers. You can seek referrals from employees, people within your networking organizations – even people you solicit. It could be that an individual has no need for your services, but it doesn't hurt to ask if they know of anyone else who does.

TAKEAWAYS:

Don't say, "There is some wiggle room." These are not the words of a closer. In fact, this tells the customer he can continue negotiating.

Don't be afraid to ask for the sale at the appropriate time. A true professional can ask several times and still not come across as being overbearing.

Act as if you do not need this sale. It is a very subtle mental attitude that conveys your confidence yet, at the same time, does not turn the customer off. This mental attitude helps keep you moving forward, and keeps you from overthinking or overhitting your next shot.

"Step In." Ask yourself: "What is the most aggressive posture I can take today to move this forward?"

Prepare and rehearse the key points and possible scenarios of major negotiations. Keep it simple and logical and know it cold going in.

Project confidence, success and prosperity throughout the closing and negotiation phases. Your posture, choice of words and tone all convey your expectation of agreement.

Where Do You Go from Here?

There has been a lot of talk about customer value throughout this book. What about salesperson value? It is a HUGE value and it is sitting there right in front of you. You, personally, are a tremendous value to your employer (but especially yourself) when you go out into the marketplace and proactively solicit new business – especially new business that has never even considered using your venue. The relationships built in these selling situations are overwhelming. They usually result in the new customer sending your general manager a letter saying (I am quoting directly from one such letter): "He worked hard to earn our business and, more importantly, delivered on every commitment. He was with us every step of the way, leaving no detail to chance. Not only do I appreciate his professionalism, I feel we have become friends."

That customer took a chance on me and the venue I worked for very early in my career. He remained a loyal customer for over 20 years, referred eight other events (four of them annual events) to me, and I used his testimonial letter countless times to close on other great pieces of business. These kind of customer relationships don't just happen, and they certainly don't happen by a chance phone or email inquiry.

Solicitation speaks to Trust, Value and Making it Happen; in other words, what it's all about for a customer. When you can show that kind of letter to another prospective customer, you have gone a long way toward answering the main question all customers have: "Why should I trust you?" As I said, testimonial letters are priceless. These are the experiences I was referring to when I asked, "Do you want to watch television on a 24" screen or a 65" plasma with surround sound"? They are just two totally different worlds.

As you can see, I am a huge proponent of proactive solicitation, and

I encourage everyone to embrace it. You will experience tremendous highs and, realistically, a few devastating lows when you enter the game. To me, it has always seemed that solicitation/networking were the only viable ways of avoiding being dragged down into the quicksand of the "illusion of selling." If you embrace solicitation and networking, you will become a much, much stronger player – an indispensable player, valued by your entire team. When you execute the strategies discussed in this book, you will be playing the game at the highest level.

You will know what it really is like as John McEnroe ("Johnny Mac") says when he is calling the play-by-play at the US Tennis Open: "You've got to dig down deep…find that other gear to get back in this match… turn things around and win it."

If you think and act more like an athlete than a salesperson, you are more than half-way there. If you are new in your job, don't look to book the type of business the venue already caters to; go out and book the type of business they don't have. Don't send emails…send letters. Don't answer the phone…pick up the phone. Don't respond…initiate. Don't fall prey to the "What ifs?" … embrace the "So whats?" Don't think… play. Come to the net, and close out the point decisively.

THE LAST QUOTE:

"It is not the critic who counts; not the man who points out how the strong man stumbles, or where the doer of deeds could have done them better. The credit belongs to the man who is actually in the arena, whose face is marred by dust and sweat and blood; who strives valiantly; who errs, who comes short again and again, because there is no effort without error and shortcoming; but who does actually strive to do the deeds; who knows the great enthusiasms, the great devotions; who spends himself in a worthy cause; who at the best knows in the end the triumph of high achievement, and who at the worst, if he fails, at least fails while daring greatly, so that his place shall never be with those cold and timid souls who neither know victory nor defeat".[52] – Theodore Roosevelt

---

[51] "The Man in the Arena" speech at the Sorbonne. Paris, France 1910.

Charles Barrett

As Director of Catering Sales at the New York Marriott Marquis in Times Square, Charlie Barrett was responsible for overall catering sales for one of New York City's largest hotels, with over 100,000 square feet of catering and meeting space.

A 34-year veteran of Marriott International, Charlie held various catering positions with the company, starting with the Stamford Marriott in 1984. He was named Director of Catering at the Westchester Marriott in 1985, and joined the opening team at the flagship New York Marriott Marquis in 1986.

Charlie has been the recipient of numerous sales achievement awards, including the highly prestigious Marriott Chairman's Circle Award, presented to the top 1 percent of the company's sales force.

His hospitality industry career began with the (then-named) Americana Hotel in New York City as Assistant Catering Sales Manager. The hotel was then purchased by the Sheraton Corporation and he was promoted to Assistant Director of Catering in 1981.Charlie remained with Sheraton for three more years before joining Marriott International.

Charlie is a graduate of Manhattan College in Riverdale, New York, where he earned a bachelor's degree in Liberal Arts. He attended the American Academy of Dramatic Arts in New York on a scholarship from the Catholic Actors Guild, where he earned an Associate Degree in Fine Arts. He is a Founder and Past President of the New York City chapter of The National Association of Catering and Events. He is a member of the Advisory Board of the Hotel Chinese Association in New York and was on the Cardinal's Committee of the Laity for the

Hospitality Industry for a number of years. He is also an active member of the parish of St. Kevin's Church.

He was honored at the Heartshare Human Services of New York annual dinner in 2010. Charlie has recently received a Special Congressional Recognition Award from Congresswoman Grace Meng for his service to the New York Asian-American Community, and was honored by the Hotel Chinese Association of New York in 2019.

A native New Yorker, Charlie and his wife Joy reside in Auburndale, Queens along with their son Tim. Charlie's sons Charles John and Christopher reside in Fairfield, and Stamford, Connecticut, respectively. Their daughter Sandra lives and works in Hong Kong.

Charlie is an avid tennis and golf player. He and his wife enjoy Ballroom and Latin dancing.

APPENDIX A

Time Management

KEYS TO MANAGING YOUR TIME

- Ask yourself each day: What are the three most important things I need to complete today? By the way, three is a magic number you can remember without a list.
- Plan tomorrow today in a quick 15 minutes. Every minute spent in planning saves about 10 minutes in execution.
- Manage or eliminate 20% of the activities that are wasting 80% of your time.
- As you go through your day, ask yourself: Could I be doing something better with my time right now?
- Your swing thought should be the importance of now and the unimportance of now.
- After 90 minutes of intense work, energy and concentration levels start to drop. High performers take 15-minute breathers every two hours. The result: they get more done at the end of the day, and it is usually higher quality work.
- Use your judgment and intuition to concentrate on the important; some things just go away if you ignore them.
- Eliminate one timewaster per week from your life.
- Eliminate "VDP" (Very Draining People) from both your work and personal life – we all know who they are!
- Do low energy tasks in low-energy periods.
- "Just Do It." Trust your instincts and judgment. You don't need everyone's approval. You can always apologize later, if

necessary._Use the: "Oh! I'm sorry, I didn't know that" or "I didn't know I couldn't do that" response. It works!

- Stop living in that fearful "What if?" zone and start living in the "So what?" zone.
- Zero in on your priorities. Act on the top 20% of activities that will create 80% of your results.

Keys to Managing Meetings

- Most meetings kill productivity, morale and time.
- Most meetings start late, include too many/the wrong people.
- Decisions are rarely made in meetings.
- Find alternatives to meetings: Cancel, postpone, conference call, delegate, telephone or email.
- At all costs, avoid being placed on an internal corporate committee. Such committees may keep "minutes" but lose hours.
- If you do attend a meeting, give it your full attention. It's rude to constantly check your watch or emails during a meeting.
- Meetings should start on time and end on time.

Keys to Managing Your Office

- **Nix the Open-Door Policy.** Ineffective team players appreciate it because they can continually come to you with their problems and you will solve them instead of their doing any thinking for themselves. The only problem is, if your door is always open, when can you get your work done? All you are really doing is being reactive and putting out fires.
- **Beware of interruptions**. Interruptions make it difficult to maintain your focus and your all-important momentum. Ask yourself: Why do I attract so many interruptions? Then act on the answers to eliminate the time wasters.
- **Manage crisis or information overload.** *Pause.* If you don't, you will be reacting all day. Take a few deep breaths, go for a walk, then come back with a fresh perspective.

- **Eliminate clutter.** Clear your work area of non-essentials. Organize it for achievement. You can't control your day if your desk is a mess.
- **Meet with influencers.** Once a week, schedule a luncheon or breakfast appointment with someone who is a "center of influence" in the business community.
- **Say "No."** Learn how to stay focused on your key goals and say no to other things. For example, when someone wants to come to your office say, "No," I will come to yours." That way you can leave when you want to.
- **Recognize co-workers' and friends' requests for what they are – demands on your time.** If someone asks if you have a few minutes to chat about something say, "No, I'm kind of under a short timeline on something right now, but I have a minute. What's up?" Deliver this one, preferably, while standing and with a smile.

APPENDIX B

The "Great Negotiator's Checklist"

- Set a hospitable, friendly and comfortable environment.
- Maintain a sincere smile and a positive and relaxed attitude, no matter how aggressive or negative the prospect becomes.
- Aim high. If you expect more, you get more.
- Make sure both you and the prospect understand each other's limits. This is critical.
- Restate objections in the form of a question.
- When an objection is presented – pause; refrain from jumping right in with a response or, worse, trying to prove you are right.
- Think of objections as requests for more information.
- Think of an objection as a sign of increased interest.
- Be prepared. Know what options you have going in.
- Avoid saying "No." Fortunately or unfortunately, almost every-thing is negotiable. If a prospective customer's request is really impossible to achieve, get around this dead-end by trading other items to compensate.
- Know you can charge more when you offer less pain and less risk.
- Establish a climate of cooperation, not conflict.
- Aim to develop relationships, not conquests.
- Do you really analyze what the customer just said (in terms of their objection) and get to what they really are saying before you speak?
- Use such language as: "It sounds like," "It looks like," "It seems like," instead of "I'm sensing that." Saying "I" too often signals to the customer you care mainly about yourself.

- If you are left with no other choice but to quote a price first, quote a broad range so you are not locked into or anchored to a lower number.
- One of the best ways to get a yes is to say yes, for example: "Yes, you have a point there" or, "Yes; I understand exactly what you are saying."
- A variation: Quote an unusual number as an end game. For example: "It will be $172.38 per person." The odd number sends a message the offer is the result of intense number crunching and, more important, that it is immoveable.
- Have prepared and practiced answers for major objections.
- React with surprise when asked for a concession.
- If you want agreement from others, be agreeable yourself.
- Document everything. If you agree to waive rental, spell it out in the confirmation, set a dollar value on it, and label it "Customer Loyalty Discount: $XX."
- Take offers/concessions off the table.
- Exhaust all alternatives before you have to say no.
- Make the potential customer work for concessions.
- Offer concessions that actually give nothing away.
- Some peoples' egos work where they think they have to get one over on you. They have to win. So, factor that into your pricing (with upgraded items) and then revise the menu using lower cost items and…let them win.
- Remember, silence is golden. Ask questions then shut up and wait for the reply.
- Stay balanced. Never let yourself feel pressured to make a concession.
- Look for and reinforce points of agreement.
- Have testimonial letters by market/industry to offer as proof you have helped people put together successful events.
- Eliminate the word "But." It is negative and implies the other party is wrong. Use "Yet" or "However."

- Call people by their first name often. It gains their attention, allows you to control the conversation, and it helps emphasize points. Besides, people like to hear the sound of their names.
- Think in terms of being loyal to customers instead of aiming for customer loyalty.
- If you are negotiating with a nervous person, speak slowly, calmly and with a sense of self-assurance.
- Ask: "What do I need to do for you to select our venue?" At a minimum, this helps get things out in the open. You don't have to agree to whatever is stated.
- Try to do your major negotiations in your high-energy periods of the day.
- Convince the other party you have another option, even if you don't.
- Make sure you always have a pipeline (prospecting funnel) full of strong leads.

Ways to Maintain a Price or Secure Higher Pricing:

- Create more benefits to compete with lower pricing.
- Be sensitive to your prospect's ego. Give a few non-price extras or services to help them over the hurdle.
- Reduce price differences to the lowest unit possible. For example: If your price is $5,000 higher than everybody else's, rephrase it as $5.00 more per person.

Common Negotiation Mistakes:

Never...

- ...match a competitive price quote. Get something before you give something.
- ...cave instead of switching products.

...sell price. Remember, you are not selling food and beverage, you are selling what it will do for them. Sell the results.

...say "Honestly." You mean you have been lying until now?

...say "Today Only"; it can put you in a bad negotiating position.

...expect negotiation to be fair. Be prepared for a take-it-or-leave-it attitude on his part, and make sure you do not reflect a similar attitude.

...make customers wait while you consult with internal decision-makers.

...use such words as: "negotiated," "reduced" or "proposed" price. It only invites more negotiation.

...use pressure to sign with such tactics as: "Menu prices are going up in one month. If you sign up now you can lock in the current price," or "I have another organization interested in the space."

...accept their first counteroffer.

...answer unasked questions

...overreact. The other venue is $35 less per person than you are! Maintain your game face. Don't let them think you are rattled. Take it on faith? No! Verify. What, exactly, is the other venue offering? They may even have to show you verifiable proof.

... make unilateral concessions. Whenever you give something, get something in return.

...make the first move. Make them state a position first. Let them outline all their demands first. They might want less than you think.

...argue. If someone is provoking you, slow down, get calm.

...apologize for higher prices.

... state this is our "policy." Everybody hates an explanation that includes the word "policy."

...say "um" or "uh." People do so more frequently when they are lying, uncertain or indecisive.

...have a pipeline (prospecting funnel) with only a few very weak leads.

About the Author

Charles Barrett worked for Marriott International for 34 years. He was Director of Catering Sales for one of the company's flagship hotels— The New York Marriott Marquis Hotel. He is a Founder and Past President of the New York chapter of Nace (National Association of Catering and Events) and he is on the Advisory Board of the Hotel Chinese Association in New York. He brings an authentic and unique perspective to learning how to be an indispensable sales performer in the world of catering and event sales.

charlie@playingtowinorafraidtolose.com

CPSIA information can be obtained
at www.ICGtesting.com
Printed in the USA
BVHW071058241019
561979BV00001B/49/P

9 781480 882386